Free Legal Aid, Theory, Legal Basis and Practice. European Standards

Ius, Lex et Res Publica
Studies in Law, Philosophy and Political Cultures

Edited by Barbara Janusz-Pohl and Anna Jaron

Volume 29

Marian Grzybowski / Bogusław Przywora /
Aleksandra Syryt (eds.)

Free Legal Aid, Theory, Legal Basis and Practice. European Standards

PETER LANG

Berlin - Lausanne - Bruxelles - Chennai - New York - Oxford

Bibliographic Information published by the Deutsche Nationalbibliothek
The Deutsche Nationalbibliothek lists this publication
in the Deutsche Nationalbibliografie; detailed bibliographic
data is available online at http://dnb.d-nb.de.

Library of Congress Cataloging-in-Publication Data
A CIP catalog record for this book has been applied for at the
Library of Congress.

Cover illustration: Courtesy of Benjamin Ben Chaim.

ISSN 2191-3250
ISBN 978-3-631-90476-3 (Print)
E-ISBN 978-3-631-91192-1 (E-Book)
E-ISBN 978-3-631-91193-8 (E-PUB)
DOI 10.3726/b21388

Published by Peter Lang GmbH, Berlin, Deutschland

info@peterlang.com - www.peterlang.com

This publication has been peer reviewed.

Table of Contents

Shortcuts

The Constitution of the Republic of Poland of 2 April 1997 (Journal of Laws No. 78, item 483, as amended) – Constitution RP

The Act of 5 August 2015 on free legal aid, free civic counseling and legal education (Journal of Laws of 2021, item 945) – Free Legal Aid Act

Constitutional Tribunal – CT

The act of 14 June 1960 Code of Administrative Procedure (Journal of Laws of 2023, item 775) – Administrative Procedure Code

European Convention for the Protection of Human Rights and Fundamental Freedoms of 4 November 1950 (Journal of Laws 1993, No. 61, item 284) – ECHR

European Court of Human Rights – ECtHR European Union – EU

The Treaty on Functioning of the European Union (EU Journal od Laws 2016/C 202/1) – TFEU

The Treaty on the European Union (EU Journal od Laws 2016/C 202/1) – TEU

The Charter of Fundamental Rights of the European Union (Journal of Laws EU C. 2007 303.1) – CRR

Introduction

In a world where more and more areas of life are covered by legal regulations, it is necessary to have legal solutions that would help navigate through specific legal systems and support the exercise of rights guaranteed by law. The point is not only to support professionals operating in political, economic or social business environment, but also to help anyone who has to shape their relations based on the law. In the latter context, the issue of free legal aid is of utmost importance. The response to contemporary challenges that result from complex law regulated mechanisms is the institution which allows people whose actual situation is indeed difficult (including those with low income, those in complicated life situations, those excluded from society due to certain character traits, or those who are discriminated) to effectively claim and protect their rights.

The *ratio legis* of free legal aid is to provide free access to legal advice at local level in order to eliminate the financial barrier in using professional legal services that exists in many countries. For this reason, the issues associated with pretrial free legal aid should be analyzed in the context where human rights are an instrument for effective assertion of freedoms and rights, especially the right to a fair trial, the right to defence, the right to challenge judgments, the right to information, the principle of social justice and the principle of equality. This issue is particularly important for direct providers of free legal aid: legal profession practitioners, NGOs, as well as the public administration units participating in the implementation (coordination) of this task, as well as central bodies responsible for the administration of justice.

The social importance of the issue of free legal aid and its various aspects, as well as its relevance in the context of human rights protection standards, have become the basis for a group of researchers from various research centers in Poland and European countries to conduct research on this phenomenon in relation to theoretical issues, and practical aspects.

The foundation of the conducted analyzes was to consider what are the existing standards that pertain to the subject, as well as to recognize whether, at the present stage of scientific discourse and practice, free legal aid may be considered an element of the right to a fair court procedure. In addition, comparative legal research was supposed to trigger a reflection on the optimal model of the free legal aid system, including its relationship with the state, local government, professional local governments performing tasks in the field of legal aid, as well as NGOs.

The authors set the following research goals:

1. to define the concept of free legal aid, taking into consideration the standards of the Council of Europe (especially those resulting from the European Convention on Human Rights and soft law standards) and the Charter of Fundamental Rights of the European Union;

2. to pinpoint solutions in the field of free legal assistance on the example of the analyzed countries: Belarus, Denmark, Spain, Germany, France, Italy, Norway, Ukraine, Poland, Switzerland, Sweden, Hungary.

The research results made it possible to prepare a monograph in which the individual authors focused on the following areas:

1. theory of free legal aid, in particular attempting to systematize the existing definitions of this concept; they also pointed out the relationship between free legal aid and education in the field of law, including the impact that teaching law has on shaping certain social attitudes and respect for the law;
2. Polish legal solutions regarding free legal aid and practices associated with the functioning of this system; it should be emphasized that most of the authors of this part participated in shaping the normative content of the free legal aid system in Poland and the standards related to its application, including prof. I. Lipowicz (Ombudsman from 2010 to 2015); retired TK judge prof. M. Grzybowski or retired Supreme Court judge prof. J. Sobczak;
3. comparative legal solutions concerning both international and local human rights protection standards (the monograph takes into account the case law of the European Court for Human Rights Protection), as well as regulations and case law of selected European countries that have experience in the field of free legal aid.

The conducted research was based on several research methods. Primarily, the logicallinguistic method was used, that facilitated determining the applicable legal norms and the legislator's will (intention) to regulate the specific, socially important state of affairs. Also, an analysis was undertaken of generally applicable legal norms of international acts and national legislation, as well as reports and information submitted by legal control and protection authorities, and legal opinions as well as recommendations regarding the provision of free legalassistance.

In order to get to know the institution of free legal aid more fully and to demonstrate solutions in the field of free legal aid – the comparative-legal method was used. This allowed to emphasize a broader perspective of the discussed considerations than the exegesis of Polish solutions alone (legal and comparative remarks on the example of several countries: Belarus, Denmark, Spain, Germany, France, Italy, Malta, Norway, Ukraine, United Kingdom, United States of America, Poland, Switzerland, Sweden, Hungary).

The historical-legal method was also applied, which made it possible to discuss the process of creating statutory regulations regarding the law on free legal assistance, including the assistance provided at the pre-trial phase.

The method of institutional analysis was also used, i.e. researching broader sources of law, that extends the traditional law researching approach by elements that enable empirical understanding of the reasons for the creation of specific legal norms as well as the socio-economic effects of their functioning.

The proposed publication is a comprehensive study on free legal aid in terms of comparative law. It deals with theoretical and practical issues that constitute a source of knowledge about the shape of legal aid in individual countries. It is also an inspiration for entities creating and applying the law to find the optimal model of free legal aid. It is composed of two volumes. In the first one in on general remarks about free legal aid and Polish solutions. The second volume describes comparative approach of the free legal aid.

This book was prepared in particular as part of the activity at the Centre for Foreign Laws of Jan Długosz University in Czestochowa and cooperation with Cardinal Stefan Wyszyński University in Warsaw.

Free legal aid – general remarks

Tomasz Barankiewicz[1]

Free prejudicial legal aid from the point of view of reaffirming the role of the state

Abstract: The paper's main purpose is to analyze free prejudicial legal aid from the point of view of the neo-Weberian thesis on reaffirming the role of the state and managerial revision and the so-called new public management. The author assumed that the performance of tasks, or more broadly, the further administration reform, could take place based on applying the principle of protecting citizens' trust in the state. The antithesis to this state is a society of risk, uncertainty and social injustice. The economic "handicap" of individuals or social groups cannot become a premise for the unavailability of basic rights. Social lack of access to the law can be identified as one of the threats to socio-economic life. The institution of free prejudicial legal aid is an important component of the perception of social life in a democratic state of law. In this respect, particular activities of the state are not charitable but represent the realization of the state's obligations towards its citizens.

Keywords: the principle of protecting citizens' trust in the state, reaffirming the state's role, state of law

1. Introduction

The subject of this study is free pre-trial legal aid analyzed from the point of view of reaffirming the role of the state, i.e., re-emphasizing its role in the new social environment. Following Ulrich Beck and Anthony Giddens, we assume that modern societies are characterized by risk and uncertainty (health, work, education, migration, exclusion). In this situation, the role of the state increases in a particular way as the guarantor of the basic rights of citizens, including access to the law (to the legal text, court, lawyers, and protection of minority groups). However, the question arises as to how the state should shape its role in order to effectively and efficiently implement the task of access to law in a society of risk and uncertainty. In response to this question, we claim that it should be a responsive state (responsive and responsive) and a state where the role of the principle of social

1 John Paul II Catholic University of Lublin. ORCID: 0000-0002-2454-1456.

trust and the principle of protection of citizens' trust in the state and law are re-emphasized. Due to the literature, the analyzes are dominated by assumptions and the sociological-legal method.

2. *Ratio legis* of the act on free legal aid, free civic counseling and legal education – a starting point for consideration

When asking in this study about the role of the modern state in the implementation of access to law as a certain social policy, or development policy, one should start with an analysis of the purpose and values that guided the authors of the Free Legal Aid Act. At the beginning, it is worth noting that the regulation, as regards the basic objective, is to form a comprehensive and coherent set of standards defining the system of free legal aid in Poland.

The full content of *ratio legis* is indicated in the rationale for the draft act in question[2]. First of all, it should be emphasized that the act is to implement Resolution No. 157 of the Council of Ministers of 25 September 2012 on the adoption of the National Development Strategy 2020, which indicates wider than before access to legal information, legal services, as well as access to legal aid for people in difficult life situations. For our considerations, the subtitle of the resolution is also important, i.e., Active Society, Competitive Economy, Efficient State, emphasizing the state's role as an important actor in the social and economic life of the country[3]. On the positive side, it can be assumed that the Act is the next stage in building a legal aid system as part of the broadly understood reform of the judiciary and the pursuit of their rights by citizens using free legal aid. On the negative side, this situation indicates that currently, citizens in the country do not have equal access to legal advice at the pre-trial stage, which is a kind of a significant axiological gap in the Polish legal system.

The axiological gap in the legal system is expressed in the fact that people with financial resources can benefit from legal aid, including legal advice at the pre-trial stage, while the lack of appropriate regulations enabling access to this type of services by persons whose financial status does not allow to cover legal advice costs. Although it can be said that in the case of free counseling, it is possible to obtain advice as part of the activities of non-governmental organizations or universities specializing in legal counseling, only residents of large urban centers can do so.

Not only from the point of view of the axiological gap but also in terms of the principle of completeness and coherence of the legal system, it can be said that the Polish legal system did not have coherent regulations that would allow natural

---

2 Justification of the government act on free legal aid, free civic counseling and legal education, http://www.sejm.gov.pl/Sejm7.nsf/druk.xsp? nr= 3338 (accessed: 15.02.2021).

3 Resolution No. 157 of the Council of Ministers of 25 September 2012 on the adoption of the National Development Strategy 2020 (Polish Monitor of 2012, item 882).

persons with low financial status to gain access to state-financed free legal aid at the pretrial stage. The possibility of obtaining free legal aid by persons who did not have the means to cover the costs of representation by an advocate or legal advisor was guaranteed only in court proceedings. In addition, the analyzed justification of the draft act assesses the legal provisions contained in the Act of 12 March 2004 on social assistance as insufficient in this respect, according to which the poviat's tasks include, among other things, providing specialist counseling, including legal counseling[4].

Finally, there are two issues worth noting. Firstly, the proposed access to legal aid at the pretrial stage is justified by the requirement of real and effective access to justice, based on a normative basis in EU law, e.g., art. 47 of the CFR and international law[5].

3. Free pre-trial legal aid and social access to law

When analyzing free pre-trial legal aid from the point of view of the role of the state, it is worth first placing this type of aid in a broader perspective of access to law in general. First of all, it should be noted that the existence of barriers to using the law and postulating various possibilities of overcoming them is a phenomenon, both historically and geographically, widespread (*semper et ubique*). The postulate of social access to law, due to various premises (equality, justice, human rights) and the search for tools to remove restrictions, is an integral element of thinking about the social order and a good state. Jan Winczorek, in his extensive study on access to law, distinguishes four social areas exercising the right, which, from the point of view of social analysis, have evolved and changed: (1) access to the legal text, (2) protection of minority groups, (3) institutional and procedural area, (4) access to lawyers in the dimension of paid and free professional legal aid[6].

The broadly understood social access to law should first be associated with the use of a legal text, the possibility of universal and effective knowledge of the sources of law, and normative acts that express citizens' rights and obligations. In this dimension, however, the law should meet not only the condition of access to the sources of law itself but also the communicativeness condition of the legal text in which the legal norms have been incorporated. A legal text, constituting a source of law, should not only be available in a direct form but also accessibility means that it is understandable, legible, and reliable for the addressees, avoiding

---

4 Art. 92 sec. 1 point 4 of the Act of 12 March 2004 on social care (Journal of Laws of 2020, item 1876 as amended).

5 For more on legal aid in the European and international perspective, see B. Przywora, *Normatywny model przedsądowej nieodpłatnej pomocy prawnej w Polsce*, Warszawa 2019, pp. 85–133; B. Przywora, A. Wróbel, *Poradnictwo obywatelskie w świetle badań prawnoporównawczych*, Warszawa 2020.

6 J. Winczorek, *Dostęp do prawa. Ujęcie socjologiczne*, Warszawa 2019, pp. 21–43.

excessive specialization of the language while in the search aspect, the legal text should be transparent in the micro and macro systematics of a normative act.

However, access to the law is revealed particularly strongly in exercising, or more precisely, the inability to exercise the right by minority groups. In this context, the problem of social exclusion appears at the stage of making and applying the law. In the process of lawmaking, minority groups most often do not have sufficient representation or sufficient political power to push for their arguments effectively. In social practice, the law can be, and unfortunately, it often happens, it becomes the law of the stronger. Meanwhile, it should be assumed that the law in social life should fulfill a compensatory and guarantee function.

We can also talk about access to law in an institutional and procedural sense. It is primarily about access to a fair trial, the right to defense and the use of a lawyer and free legal aid in the judicial process of applying the law. In this dimension, there are many institutions and procedures for access to law that implement the principle of equality and social justice, such as institutions of an ombudsman character (Ombudsman, Ombudsman for Children, Ombudsman for Patients' Rights), or general rules of administrative proceedings that are imposed on an authority the public's duty to inform about the legal situation of citizens affecting their rights and obligations.

And finally, it will be the area of social access to lawyers and thus obtaining professional legal aid. Legal historians emphasize that the emergence of legal professions and the provision of legal services should be associated with the right of access to courts and the process of formalization and conventionalization. Speaking of access to law as access to lawyers may generally be about being professionally represented by a lawyer before a court, and also about access to a lawyer when the costs of a representation by the court are covered by the state. When we talk about access to lawyers in the context of free legal aid, we usually mean the second of the indicated meanings, when the costs of exercising a power of attorney are covered by the state.

The above-mentioned short analysis allows to define the characteristics of the area of free pretrial legal aid, its axiology and, above all, the fundamental role of the state in building real and effective possibilities of free legal aid. In addition, from the point of view of sociological analysis, it is about the obligation of the state to protect minority groups, on the basis of such values as equality, justice, and human right. However, another question arises as to whether the modern state, socio-political systems and social policies cope with the process of permanent recognition of minority groups or social exclusion groups and create appropriate means of effectively providing free pre-trial legal aid. It is therefore a question of seeking an effective and efficient system of free legal aid.

4. The role of the state in the face of risk, uncertainty and social exclusion

Looking for an answer to the above question whether the modern state copes with the problem of access to the right of minority groups, let us assume, following U. Beck and A. Giddens, that contemporary societies can be defined as the so-called risk and uncertainty society[7].

The argument shared by the author after U. Beck and A. Giddens is based on the fact that in a situation of increasing risk and uncertainty, the role of the state, also in relation to the area of minority groups in access to law, has increased significantly. The following areas of contemporary social risk and uncertainty are indicated: risk in the area of the natural environment; health risk; the risk of losing a job or seeking only temporary work and quick profit; education risk without job security; diminishing importance of tradition, customs and permanent socio-cultural norms; expanding area of possibilities and individual choice; financial and economic risk; uncertainty of political options; marriage insecurity; the risk and uncertainty of the future due to new requirements, trends, standards and technologies[8].

Risk and uncertainty have constantly accompanied human life, so the question arises what characterizes contemporary risk and uncertainty. In the case of modern societies, we do not mean any kind of natural risk. It is about man-made risk, which is a consequence of the civilization achievements of Western culture.

There are three causes that generate risk and uncertainty today. First of all, an increasing number of new technical solutions, including biotechnological ones, have appeared in the process of modernizing human life. The interaction of man, technology and the environment has become unpredictable. The second reason is the increase in opportunities in the area of individual choices, as well as the understanding of man as free in making life choices. In social life, where the freedom of the individual is one of the basic values, we are faced with a much wider than before area of possible implementation of individual plans. As a consequence, the path of further development and the future become unpredictable. It is difficult to indicate the necessary conditions for further development. Large areas of social and economic life become perceptually impossible to monitor continuously. Therefore, not having complete and constant information needed to make appropriate choices, the public authority, in its traditional understanding, naturally loses the ability to effectively manage the whole. A specific dysfunction of the state appears as a specific structure that has full knowledge of social threats and expectations. This requires a new look at the role of the state "here and now". And the third

---

7 U. Beck, *Risikogesellschaft – Auf dem Weg in eine andere Moderne*, Frankfurt am Main 1986 (*Społeczeństwo ryzyka. W drodze do innej nowoczesności*, transl. S. Cieśla, Warszawa 2002); A. Giddens, *Socjologia*, Warszawa 2008, p. 87.

8 A. Giddens, *Socjologia*, Warszawa 2008, pp. 87–95.

reason is the nature of social decisions which, due to the principle of public debate in a deliberative democracy, are only temporary, which leads to the phenomenon of a permanent state of risk[9].

The uncertainty of the development of future events causes that the risk has become a common category. Risk and uncertainty apply to everyone today, regardless of social position, profession, level of education, wealth and place of residence.

Contemporary sociological thought in terms of the society of risk and uncertainty, however, is not negative. If, on the one hand, we can talk about uncertainty and risk, on the other hand, the moment of transition from the traditional to a new shape and a new method of collective life is emphasized, when risk management by public authorities will play an important role. This reaffirms the role of the state and public authority. Not in the sense of interfering with the private sphere of citizens, but activities in the field of social communication, monitoring the social situation and risk calculation, with various possible plans for maintaining safety (A, B, C ...)[10]. This concept implies changes in the sphere of thinking about the non-authoritarian state, but its main function is to protect and guarantee the rights of citizens[11].

5. Rediscovery of social trust and its institutional protection

A review of the literature on the subject indicates the rediscovery of the phenomenon of social and institutional trust, which is part of an attempt at a new look at the role of the state, directing its mission, inter alia, to protect citizens' trust in state institutions and public authorities[12]. Therefore, it is worth taking a closer look at the phenomenon of natural and institutional trust, which, as U. Beck and A. Giddens claim earlier, may be an answer in coping with social risk and uncertainty, including the risk of social exclusion.

The natural phenomenon of trust in people can be understood as trust shown in private life and in life with other people in social relationships. This type of trust can also be described as primary, natural or personal. This type of trust allows us to

---

9 Ibidem, pp. 96–98; see also: T. Barankiewicz, *Neoweberyzm. Etos służby publicznej*, Lublin 2020, pp. 16–23; P. Kaczmarek, *Działanie w instytucji w teoriach społecznych późnej nowoczesności*, [in:] K. J. Kaleta, P. Skuczyński (eds.), *Refleksyjność w prawie. Konteksty i zastosowania*, Warszawa 2015, pp. 229–252.

10 M. Pichlak, *Refleksyjność prawa. Od teorii społecznej do strategii regulacji i z powrotem*, Łódź 2019, pp. 137–154.

11 Ibidem.

12 P. Sztompka, *Zaufanie. Fundament społeczeństwa*, Kraków 2007, pp. 45–50; See also M. Stahl, M. Kasiński, K. Wlaźlak, *Sprawiedliwość i zaufanie do władz publicznych w prawie administracyjnym*, Warszawa 2015. The publication is an extensive aftermath of the 5th conference of the Lodz Legal Meetings.

introduce a reasonable belief as to a specific future course of life-important matters. People's actions based on a relationship of trust become more flexible, they do not require constant risk calculations. Trust in the personal sense does not exclude a situation in which people compete for better results with other participants in social life. At the same time, it is important to maintain the accepted principles of an honest and socially expected course of action.

Our deliberations on the risk, uncertainty and re-affirmation of the role of the state, however, focus on institutional trust, i.e., trust in public institutions and the methods and standards of public authority operation required in this regard.

In traditional societies, we faced the existing constructions of the world, real and social, nowadays the world and social life are treated as something open, changeable and often unforeseeable. The concept of a society of many possibilities, and at the same time a risk society, influences the assessments and expectations of society in relation to the state as an important actor in social life. In this new context, the importance of social trust in its institutional dimension increase. Although it is a kind of trust derived from natural trust, in a society of risk and uncertainty it acquires special importance, along with the role of the state. This does not mean that personal trust will become something secondary and unnecessary, but rather this process should be perceived as a new area of social trust, complementary, having the dimension of protecting natural trust, as the basic social bond[13].

In the global world, even distant factors and people influence each other, hence the role of trust in systems is changing. Using water, food, electricity and fuel every day, we do not know directly the institutions that provide us with these goods of appropriate, as we assume, quality and in the right, expected time. The same applies to trust in the institutions of the state and the law. As we have to rely more and more on "abstract systems", the importance of social trust in its institutional dimension increases[14].

6. Conclusions

The model of the society-state relationship proposed by U. Beck and A. Giddens does not fit in with the concept of the so-called a minimal state, which severely limits the social welfare system, or in the model of a maximum state, whose welfare system is strongly developed. It is rather about the so-called the model of a responsive state, when the public authority reacts, responds and creates a strategy for counteracting social exclusion in the processes of monitoring social phenomena, communication and political debate. In addition, and importantly, in this sense, we should also talk about the rediscovery of the relationship of social trust

---

13 D. Miłoszewicz, *Zaufanie jako wartość społeczna*, „Studnia Ekonomiczne. Zeszyty Naukowe Uniwersytetu Ekonomicznego w Katowicach" 2016, no. 259, pp. 80–88.

14 M. Wojciechowski, *Zaufanie instytucjonalne w kontekście zaufania jednostki do państwa*, „Ruch Prawniczy, Ekonomiczny i Socjologiczny" 2012, no. 2, pp. 7–17.

and citizens' institutional trust in public authorities, and protection of this trust by public authorities when applying the law.

Literature

Barankiewicz T., *Neoweberyzm. Etos służby publicznej*, Lublin 2020.

Beck U., *Risikogesellschaft – Auf dem Weg in eine andere Moderne*, Frankfurt am Main 1986 (*Społeczeństwo ryzyka. W drodze do innej nowoczesności*, tłum. S. Cieśla, Warszawa 2002).

Giddens A., *Socjologia*, Warszawa 2008.

Kaczmarek P., *Działanie w instytucji w teoriach społecznych późnej nowoczesności*, [in:] K. J. Kaleta, P. Skuczyński (eds.), *Refleksyjność w prawie. Konteksty i zastosowania*, Warszawa 2015.

Miłoszewicz D., *Zaufanie jako wartość społeczna*, „Studnia Ekonomiczne. Zeszyty Naukowe Uniwersytetu Ekonomicznego w Katowicach" 2016, no. 259.

Pichlak M., *Refleksyjność prawa. Od teorii społecznej do strategii regulacji i z powrotem*, Łódź 2019.

Przywora B., *Normatywny model przedsądowej nieodpłatnej pomocy prawnej w Polsce*, Warszawa 2019.

Przywora B., Wróbel A., *Poradnictwo obywatelskie w świetle badań prawnoporównawczych*, Warszawa 2020.

Stahl M., Kasiński M., Wlaźlak K., *Sprawiedliwość i zaufanie do władz publicznych w prawie administracyjnym*, Warszawa 2015.

Sztompka P., *Zaufanie. Fundament społeczeństwa*, Kraków 2007.

Winczorek J., *Dostęp do prawa. Ujęcie socjologiczne*, Warszawa 2019.

Wojciechowski M., *Zaufanie instytucjonalne w kontekście zaufania jednostki do państwa*, „Ruch Prawniczy, Ekonomiczny i Socjologiczny" 2012, no. 2.

Karol Dobrzeniecki[1]

Access to justice for the poor as a well-established legal value and a goal of legal reform in transitional and developing countries

Abstract: Since the turn of the Middle Ages and the early modern era, the importance of equal access to justice and the need to provide legal aid to the most demanding members of society have been recognized. Throughout history, rulers have tried to provide them in various ways. The author presents in a synthetic way how Western countries came to recognize equity of justice as a fundamental legal value and presents the assumptions of programs supporting the dissemination of this value in the legal systems of developing countries in the twenty-first century.

Keywords: legal aid, access to justice, legal empowerment, rule of law, the poor

1. Introduction

Post-war programs of legal reform usually promoted strengthening rule of law institutions through technical assistance and development of policy and tools to build capacity and enhance skills of the judiciary. In this approach investigatory and prosecutorial capabilities were to be enhanced in areas such as organized crime, anti-corruption, cybercrime, money laundering etc. With the popularization of the welfare state model, greater importance began to be attached to equal access to the justice system. "A huge expansion of legal aid programs took place during the 1960s and 1970s, and then, a major contraction during the 1980s and 1990s"[2]. This retreat was influenced by the change in social and economic policy in the spirit of neoliberalism, which took place in the United States and Europe. Great emphasis was placed on the issue of "smaller government", which limited the funds allocated to social programs. At the beginning of the twenty-first

1 Nicolaus Copernicus University in Toruń. ORCID: 0000-0002-6364-9793.
2 S. Armstrong, *What has happened to legal aid?*, „University of Western Sydney Law Review" 2001, vol. 5 no. 1, p. 91.

century under the influence of the global struggle against poverty, legal reform programs have again "shifted their focus to the justice seeker, in particular the poor and the marginalized, in particular women and indigenous people. This shift from top-down institutional reform to bottom-up intervention informs the new focus on access to justice and the new strategy of legal empowerment"[3]. Many influential organizations conceptualize access to justice and legal empowerment reforms with particular emphasis on this issue. Among them there are the Ford Foundation, the Asian Development Bank (ADB), the United Nations Development Programme, the World Bank, the UK Department for International Development (DfID), Penal Reform International and the Commission for Legal Empowerment of the Poor (CLEP). In a 2008 study prepared by The Center of Expertise on Rule of Law and Development at the request of the Netherlands Ministry of Foreign Affairs in 2008, two directions of the desired reform of law in developing countries were indicated. They are defined as: access to justice reform and legal empowerment reform. "Access to justice reforms focus on poor and marginalized people's lack of access to law and the legal system, which effectively deprives them of their ability to enjoy and protect their rights. Efforts at legal empowerment focus on the lack of power, opportunities and capacities that impede poor and marginalized people's use of law and (para) legal tools to take control of their lives and improve their livelihoods"[4]. Later in the text I will point out how Western countries have come to recognize equity of justice as a fundamental legal value, and I will also present the assumptions of programs supporting the dissemination of this value in the legal systems of developing countries.

2. Equality of justice: A fundamental value in the Western legal culture

The problem of access to justice by people from the lower social classes was updated in Western Europe with the breakthrough that took place in the legal sphere at the turn of the Middle Ages and modern times. At that time, there was a phenomenon of an increased search for legal protection in formal court proceedings, also in small cases that had not previously been brought to the courts. "Medieval and early modern rulers commonly proclaimed that protecting the legal entitlements of the personae miserabiles, who included widows, orphans, the chronically ill and 'the poor', was among their principal duties. The entitlement of the poor to legal services was not a matter of grace but was in fact their 'good right'. For example, widows, orphans, and other *personae miserabili* had the privilege of being heard in first instance before high courts, so as to save time and costs in pursuing their legal claims. Another example of manifest commitment to legal entitlement for the poor

3 I. van de Meene, B. van Rooij, *Access to justice and legal empowerment making the poor central in legal development co-operation*, Leiden 2008, p. 6.
4 Ibidem, p. 7.

was the refusal of Philip II of Habsburg to consent to measures that would limit the jurisdiction of his Castilian chanceries; the measures had been proposed so as to limit the chanceries' ever-increasing workload, but, because they could also restrict indigents' access to such courts, were rejected by the monarch"[5].

In practice, the problem of access to justice by the poor has not been solved in the modern era, both in the Old and New Worlds. Historically legal aid originates in the right to counsel and right to a fair trial movement of the nineteenth-century continental European countries. "Poor man's laws" reduced court fees for the poor and provided for the appointment of duty solicitors for those who could not afford to pay for legal service.

"Justice and the Poor" is a book written in 1919 by American lawyer Reginald Heber Smith. It presents the first history of the development of legal aid societies in US and concludes with a call for the bar and society to provide access to the legal system for people who cannot afford attorneys. That is the necessary condition of the proper development of the law which addresses the needs of all people and will guarantee that the poor are able to vindicate their rights through use of the legal system. His postulate was to increase the number of legal aid societies, ensure that they are properly funded, and advocate for the rights of the impoverished. Smith's fundamental claim was that access to the courts is rooted in the obligation of justice. „Freedom and equality of justice are twin fundamental conceptions of American jurisprudence. Together they form the basic principle on which our entire plan for the administration of justice is built. They are so deep-rooted in the body and spirit of our laws that the very meaning which we ascribe to the word justice embraces them"[6]. He also argued that because equality of justice is a fundamental part of American jurisprudence, guaranteeing it is the essential role of government. Finally, according to Smith a democratic system of government which fails to so secure equality of justice for citizens itself becomes endangered. "To withhold the equal protection of the laws, or to fail to carry out their intent by reason of inadequate machinery, is to undermine the entire structure and threaten it with collapse"[7].

In 1940 American lawyer Sidney B. Jacoby claimed that "equal protection of law is the cornerstone of our system of living. 'Equality under the law', 'one law for the rich and the poor' are mottoes we greatly pride ourselves, and undoubtedly, we do so with sincerity and a sense of grateful security."[8] At present equal justice under law is declared as a fundamental American value. Legal aid includes direct legal advocacy, representation and legal information. Direct services can be

5 R. H. Smith, *Justice and the poor. A study of the present denial of justice to the poor and of the agencies making more equal their position before the law, with particular reference to legal aid work in the United States*, New York 1919, p. 3.
6 S. B. Jacoby, *Legal aid to the poor*, "Harvard Law Review" 1940, vol. 53, no. 6, p. 940.
7 Ibidem, p. 5.
8 Journal of Laws of 2020, item 755 as amended.

representation by legal aid staff attorneys or volunteers from private law firms. Legal advice is provided to help identify legal issues and possible solutions. In the United States legal aid is primarily funded through three sources. At the federal level it is a Legal Services Corporation which provides funding for civil legal aid to low-income individuals with and without disabilities. At the private level, the interest from the lawyers' trust accounts (IOLTA) is pooled to provide civil legal aid to the poor. At the state level funding is provided by state legislatures.

According to some authors, the assessment of the legal protection of the poorest in the United States one hundred years after the publication of Smith's book still leaves much to be desired.

> Presently, funding for legal aid programs, including government funded programs, continues to decrease. Legal aid attorneys continue to be dramatically underpaid and are expected to carry monstrous caseloads. These fluctuations in funding and the various private and public mechanisms for providing legal services have left the poor in substantially the same position as Smith found them in 1919, with limited access to the American justice system and very little advocacy for law reform[9].

Legal aid systems exist in all Member States of the EU in both civil and criminal proceedings. It allows those who do not have sufficient financial resources to meet the costs of a court case or legal representation.

For example, in the Republic of Poland, there is a system of state guarantees aimed at ensuring access to legal aid for the poor in cases heard by courts. The system of these guarantees has a clear constitutional basis in the case of the right to defense (art. 42 (2) of the Constitution RP: "Anyone against whom criminal proceedings have been brought shall have the right to defense at all stages of such proceedings. He may, in particular, choose counsel or avail himself – in accordance with principles specified by statute – of counsel appointed by the court.") These powers are related in the doctrine and jurisprudence with the implementation of the constitutional right to a fair trial. Art. 45 (1) of the Constitution RP provides that "everyone shall have the right to a fair and public hearing of his case, without undue delay, before a competent, impartial and independent court".

The literature indicates that the possibility of appointing an attorney representing the interest of a participant in the proceedings or exemption from court costs is important for ensuring that the parties (legal entities) have access to court in order to protect their rights. Such guarantees allow for judicial protection to be granted to disadvantaged entities, for whom it is not possible to bear the costs of legal aid or court costs without prejudice to the necessary subsistence[10].

The right to appoint an attorney (defense attorney) ex officio or to be exempted from the costs of the proceedings is granted only to the poor, for whom incurring

9 Journal of Laws of 2019, item 540 as amended.

10 *Kodeks postępowania cywilnego. Komentarz*, K. Piasecki (ed.), vol. I, Warszawa 2001, p. 515.

the costs of such legal aid or paying the costs would be a detriment to the necessary subsistence. Judicial case law emphasizes the impossibility of defining abstractly the content of the concept of "necessary maintenance". It is indicated, for example, that only in the context of a specific case, with a comprehensive assessment of the personal and financial situation of a participant in the proceedings, the legitimacy of the exemption from court costs and its scope (full or partial).

In the judgment of 5 March 1959 (4 CZ 25/59), the Supreme Court stated that the right to exemption from costs was not granted to everyone, but to people who really need it. The court noted that a party intending to bring a case to court should consider the necessity to incur certain expenses and save for this purpose, limiting the satisfaction of current needs. "Only when the making of these savings would lead to a clear detriment to the necessary livelihood of the party and the family, can we speak of the existence of a basis for granting an exemption".

In the Republic of Poland, obtaining legal aid ex officio is possible both within the framework of criminal proceedings (appointment of an ex officio defender or attorney of the injured party, as well as exemption from court costs), civil proceedings (exemption from court costs and appointment of an attorney or legal advisor) or court proceedings administrative (the so-called law of assistance). The defendant (suspect), who does not have a defense lawyer by choice, may demand that he be appointed a public defense lawyer, if he duly proves that he is unable to bear the costs of defense without prejudice to the necessary support for himself and his family. Pursuant to the Act of July 28, 2005 on court costs in civil cases[11] an exemption from court costs may be requested by a natural person, if he or she submits a declaration that shows that he or she is unable to bear them without prejudice to the maintenance necessary for himself and his family, or incurring them will expose him to such detriment. The application for exemption from court costs should be accompanied by a declaration containing detailed data on the family status, property, income and sources of income of the person applying for exemption from costs. In proceedings before administrative courts, the right to assistance may be granted to a party upon its application submitted before the proceedings are instituted or in the course of the proceedings. The right of assistance includes exemption from court costs and the appointment of an attorney, legal advisor, tax advisor or patent attorney (art. 244 § 1 of the Law on Proceedings before Administrative Courts) and may be granted in full or in part. Act of 14 February 1991 Law on Notaries[12] provides that in a situation where a party to a notarial act is unable, without prejudice to the maintenance necessary for himself and his family, to

---

11 See: judgments of the CT of 1 December 2008, P 54/07, OTK ZU No. 10/A/2008, item 171; 31 March 2009, SK 19/08, OTK ZU No. 3/A/2009, item. 29; 15 November 2016, SK 46/15, OTK ZU A/2016, item 87.

12 S. Golub, *The legal empowerment alternative*, [in:] T. Carothers (ed.), *Promoting the rule of law abroad. In search of knowledge*, Washington, D.C. 2006, pp. 161–187, Carnegie Endowment for International Peace, 2006, p. 161.

bear the remuneration demanded by the notary, he may apply to the district court having jurisdiction over his place of residence for exemption in whole or in part from paying this remuneration (art. 6 § 1). The Act of 28 February 2018 on bailiff fees provides that a party who is a natural person who does not benefit from the statutory exemption from court costs and has not been exempted from these costs in the examination proceedings, and at the same time is not able to maintain the necessary for himself and the family to incur bailiff's expenses or fees, the payment of which depends on the bailiff taking action, may apply to the district court at which the bailiff operates for an exemption from these costs in whole or in part (art. 45 (1) and (3)).

In the judgment of 20 November 2019 (SK 6/18), the Constitutional Tribunal upheld its earlier position that granting an attorney ex officio always constitutes the exercise of the right to social security, resulting from art. 67 of the Constitution RP[13]. This provision reads as follows: "Art. 67.1. A citizen shall have the right to social security whenever incapacitated for work by reason of sickness or invalidism as well as having attained retirement age. The scope and forms of social security shall be specified by statute 2. A citizen who is involuntarily without work and has no other means of support, shall have the right to social security, the scope of which shall be specified by statute".

The aforementioned constitutional provision covers all benefits granted from public funds to a citizen in a difficult personal and financial situation, but it is not possible to derive a constitutional right to any specific form of benefit from it (judgment of the CT of 1 April 2008, SK 96/06). Also, the Polish Supreme Court in the resolution of 21 September 2000, III CZP 14/00, stated that "in our legal system (unlike in many other countries), both the need to provide a poor person with social assistance in the form of exemption from court costs due to the state, and the appointment of a lawyer, are not decided by the authorities, whose task is to provide this assistance, but the courts". In the judgment of 12 May 2011, P 38/08, the Court held that the exemption from court fees is not an administration of justice in the literal sense, but rather an activity in the field of administering budgetary funds and may be entrusted to highly qualified court officials, providing the party with the possibility of lodging a complaint against the referendary's decision to the court[14]. The legal doctrine previously held a similar position[15]. The Tribunal found that entrusting officials (in Poland called "court referendaries") with the issue of exemption from costs is a step towards taking this matter out of court, and even outside the Ministry of Justice, and in the future decisions in this matter should not be taken by the court (judge), but other state or local government body, e.g.

13 I. van de Meene, B. van Rooij, op. cit., p. 14.

14 I. van de Meene, B. van Rooij, op. cit., p. 6–9.

15 See A. M. Arkuszewska, *Referendarz sądowy – status i uprawnienia*, „Radca Prawny“ 2006, no. 5, p. 74.

a social welfare (welfare) institution that knows the situation of poor people who need such help.

3. Access to justice and legal empowerment

The term access to justice is accompanied by the term legal empowerment. By definition "legal empowerment is the use of legal services, often in combination with related development activities, to increase disadvantaged populations' control over their lives. It is both an alternative to the problematic, state-centric rule-of-law orthodoxy and a means of making rights-based development a reality by using law to support broader socioeconomic development initiatives"[15].

Most often, the expression "legal empowerment" is treated as a social supplement to the liberal postulate of universal access to court. Legal empowerment approach prioritizes civil society support because that is typically the best route to strengthening the legal capacities and power of the poor[16]. Justice for the poor means need for demand oriented, community driven approach to justice and governance reform, which values the perspectives of the users, particularly the poor and marginalized as women, youth, and ethnic minorities[17].

4. A new direction of law reform in developing countries

Access to justice and legal empowerment constitute a new trend in legal development cooperation. The poor and marginalized face obstacles in seeking justice and empowerment through the legal system. According to the note published by The Centre of Expertise on Rule of Law and Development most approaches to the reforms share the same general features. They are as follows:

"- Access to justice and legal empowerment are sensitive areas with political limitations
- Conceptual focus on dispute settlement ignores the prevention of grievances
- Reforms need to address both state and non-state justice systems
- Both state a civil society must play a role
- Access to justice and legal empowerment in criminal cases should include both the victim and the defendant
- Setting realistic goals, prioritization and coordination prevent disappointment
- Entry points and sequencing reform are context-related
- Measuring outcome and impact is essential"[18].

One of the examples of such programs is The Justice for the Poor (J4P) initiative funded by the World Bank. It is aimed at promoting legitimate and equitable

16 Ibidem.

17 See B. v. Rooij, *Bringing justice to the poor: Bottom-up legal development cooperation*, "Hague Journal on the Rule of Law" 2012, v. 4, p. 286.

systems to manage conflict arising from development. In partnership with the Australian Department of Foreign Affairs and Trade, the program "engages in analytical and operational work to support the emergence of socially embedded institutions to increase access to justice and manage conflicts related to land, natural resources and public spending on goods and services"[18].

5. Conclusions

In general, legal aid is essential to guaranteeing equal access to justice for all. Civil legal aid helps ensure fairness in the justice system, regardless of how much money one has. For citizens who do not have sufficient financial means, the provision of legal aid to clients by governments increases the likelihood, within court proceedings, of being assisted by legal professionals for free or at a lower cost, or of receiving financial aid. In the last decade, the belief that access to justice and legal empowerment are essential in the fight against poverty has spread among international organizations. Reforms informed by such approaches "support poor and marginalized people in their efforts to seek and obtain justice and to use the legal system to improve their lives"[20].

Literature

Arkuszewska A. M., *Referendarz sądowy – status i uprawnienia*, „Radca Prawny" 2006, no. 5.

Armstrong S., *What has happened to legal aid?*, "University of Western Sydney Law Review" 2001, vol. 5 no. 1.

DiPippa J. M. A., *Reginald Heber Smith and justice and the poor in the 21st century*, "Campbell Law Review" 2018, vol. 40, issue 1.

Golub S., *The legal empowerment alternative*, [in:] T. Carothers (ed.), *Promoting the rule of law abroad: In search of knowledge*, Washington, D.C. 2006.

Jacoby S. B., *Legal aid to the poor*, "Harvard Law Review" 1940, vol. 53, no. 6.

Kodeks postępowania cywilnego. Komentarz, K. Piasecki (ed.), vol. I, Warszawa 2001.

Rooij V., *Bringing justice to the poor: Bottom-up legal development cooperation*, "Hague Journal on the Rule of Law" 2012, vol. 4.

Smith R. H., *Justice and the poor: A study of the present denial of justice to the poor and of the agencies making more equal their position before the law, with particular reference to legal aid work in the United States*, New York 1919.

Van de Meene I., Van Rooij B., *Access to justice and legal empowerment making the poor central in legal development co-operation*, Leiden 2008.

---

18 The World Bank website, https://www.worldbank.org/en/topic/governance/brief/justice-for-the-poor, (accessed 22.03.2021).

Vermeesch G., *Access to justice: Legal aid to the poor at civil law courts in the eighteenth-century low countries*, "Law and History Review" 2014, vol. 32, no. 3.

Agnieszka Klimska[1] and Aleksandra Syryt[2]

The concept and significance of legal education

Abstract: The assumption of the study is to demonstrate that legal education is part of civic education. Its purpose is, as a first priority, to adopt measures leading to raising the legal awareness of the society. In the wake of this fact, based on the literature dedicated to pedagogy and legal sciences, the authors will reconstruct the definition of the term "legal education" and explain how it fits into the phenomenon of civic education. Starting from the assumption that a person with high legal awareness and culture will not only seek the protection of their rights, but also will not violate the rights and freedoms of others, the impact of legal education on respect for the legal system and the correct approach of individuals to shaping this system will be described.

Keywords: legal education, civic education, legal culture

1. Introduction

The concept of legal education can have two dimensions. First, it may concern the training of lawyers. In today's complex and rapidly changing world, legal education stands as a vital pillar in nurturing competent legal professionals who possess not only a deep understanding of the law but also the necessary skills to apply it effectively. Legal education encompasses a range of educational programs and activities, including undergraduate, graduate, and professional programs, designed to equip individuals with the knowledge, skills, and ethical values required to succeed in the legal field. Secondly, legal education can be analyzed in a broader context, as the transfer of knowledge about the law to the public, which must function within a specific legal framework. Education of law, as an integral component of civic education, holds immense importance in fostering an informed and engaged citizenry. Education plays a crucial role in equipping individuals with the knowledge and skills needed to participate meaningfully in society and exercise their rights and responsibilities as citizens. Within the realm of civic education,

1 Cardinal Stefan Wyszyński University in Warsaw. ORCID: 0000-0002-9115-9492.
2 Cardinal Stefan Wyszyński University in Warsaw. ORCID: 0000-0002-7501-0786.

education of law emerges as a fundamental pillar, enabling individuals to comprehend the legal system, engage with legal processes, and understand the rights and obligations inherent in democratic societies.

In this text, an attempt will be made to indicate the concept of legal education in particular in the second of the above-mentioned meanings, as well as to determine its meaning. The findings will be made on the basis of an analysis of literature in the field of pedagogy, law, sociology, as well as auxiliary on the basis of normative acts.

2. Definition

Legal education can be understood in two ways. In a narrow sense, it is defined as legal studies, related to the academic training of future lawyers and the improvement of the legal profession through specialized education, such as legal applications. In a broad sense, legal education is defined as a component of civic education and is independent of the profession. It encompasses all kinds of endeavors aimed at different social groups. The starting point for this proposal is to provide basic knowledge of law – legal principles and the legal order – in order to raise the legal awareness of its recipients. The Free Legal Aid Act specifies that this type of education concerns the dissemination of knowledge about: civic rights and obligations, the activities of national and international legal protection bodies, mediation and ways of amicable dispute resolution, opportunities for citizens to participate in public consultations and the law-making process, as well as access to free legal aid and free civic counseling.

Following V. Kopinska, it can be assumed that the fundamental task of legal education to develop of the individual/group enabling him/her to gain the highest possible awareness of the legal regulations in force in the communities to which they belong. In addition, the aim is to awaken the legal creativity of the individual so that they can not only respect the law but also create it. A further important aspect is to make individuals aware of the importance of legal action that goes beyond the threshold of ad hoc or self-interest[3]. The author refers to Z. Kwieciński and draws attention to two particularly important aspects of legal education: education and legal deification, understood as the shaping and implementation of legal consciousness and the assumption of civic activities and roles. According to V. Kopinska, one must be careful not to identify legal education with legal deification[4].

Legal education should seek to develop skills. Focusing only on the transmission of knowledge hinders development and multiplies the problems present in social life. Therefore, legal education should be seen from a humanistic-critical

3 V. Kopinska, *Legal education from a humanistic-critical perspective*, "Andragogical Yearbook", T. 19/2012, p. 190.

4 Ibidem, p. 189.

perspective, building both adaptive and emancipatory-critical capacities.[5] Adaptive ones involve the acquisition of a certain fluency or proficiency in a certain action or behavior, the disposition and motivation for this action and the adaptation to the environment[6]. Emancipatory-critical competence, on the other hand, refers to the subject's ability to act creatively and analyze the social context of action and think critically[7].

Education is one of the key mechanisms of development, and therefore the transmission of sound legal knowledge should also be considered a priority. One should be aware that "(...) problems generated by the modern world contribute to the complexity of educational tasks and the pace of changes occurring in social, economic and political spheres (...) require immediate actions aimed at raising social awareness of the risks involved. The crisis affecting the education sector, which is a global problem in today's world, is an obstacle to this."[8]. Education, including legal education, must therefore keep abreast of current events and trends in a dynamically changing reality, and involve individuals in active participation in society. Studies show that the legal awareness of Poles is low[9]. This results in an inability to defend their rights effectively, on the one hand, and the risk of being in conflict with the law, on the other. The legal awareness of citizens is one of the determinants of development and a responsible attitude of society. Individuals seeking to solve their problems should use legal tools and have knowledge of basic procedures and applicable laws[10]. Modern legal education must consider not only the problem of how a person functions in legal reality due to the variability of the law or the specificity of language. The challenge for this education is to answer the questions of the meaning of law for human beings, the creator of law, the purpose and means of its creation, its scope (local or global) and the question of ambivalence between unanimity and diversity in law. Legal education is the most effective tool for creating legal awareness by providing knowledge and, at the same time, competences to function in a changing society. D. Woźniakowska-Fajst points out that the legal awareness of society is formed by a coherent system, which consists of legal education, legal information and legal counseling[11]. Legal education should

---

5 Ibidem, p. 194.

6 R. Góralska, H. Solarczyk-Szewc, *On competences in the context of the Polish Qualifications Framework for lifelong learning*, "Edukacja Dorosłych", 2(67)/2021, p. 29.

7 M. Czerepaniak-Walczak, *Emancipatory pedagogy: The development of human critical consciousness*, Gdańsk 2006, p. 130.

8 M. Klimski, *Call for high quality education in the context of the postmodern society conception*, 'Zeszyty Naukowe Politechniki Śląskiej. Series: Organization and Management', 2018/z. 122, p. 83.

9 M. Boczek, *Legal awareness of Poles as a challenge of the 21st century*, [in:] D. Gierszewski, H. A. Kretek (eds.), *Adult civic education and civil society*, Racibórz 2015.

10 A. Dudak, *The essence and importance of legal education in shaping an open society*, "Pedagogical Review" 2/2014, pp. 66. 65–73.

11 D. Woźniakowsk-Fajst, *Legal education – opportunities, chances, barriers*, INPRIS Foundation, Warsaw 2012, p. 12.

be implemented in schools from the earliest years, as well as extra-institutionally, informally and universally through adult education. Indeed, in this system, legal education is the first stage in which it is assumed that the citizen will be equipped with knowledge of general legal principles. On the other hand, legal information, usually in the form of brochures, leaflets and handbooks, helps to solve specific problems. It results from the activities of entities, e.g., non-governmental organizations, publishing houses, parliamentary offices, and makes it possible to broaden knowledge in the scope and topic of interest. Counseling refers to situations in which expert help is used to solve a problem. Legal education therefore equips citizens to seek and use legal information and advice. The implementation and promotion of this education are also legitimate and necessary for preventive reasons, such as counteracting social exclusion. In addition, legal education contributes to the growth of a legal culture, which consists of "(…) socially accepted patterns that foster solutions leading to balance and a sense of justice"[12].

3. Features of legal education

Education of law, as a subset of civic education, focuses on providing individuals with an understanding of legal principles, systems, and processes. It encompasses the teaching and learning of legal knowledge, skills, and values, enabling individuals to navigate legal complexities, uphold the rule of law, and actively participate in democratic governance. Education of law not only equips citizens with legal literacy but also fosters a sense of civic responsibility, empowering them to protect their rights, advocate for justice, and contribute to the betterment of their communities[13].

The primary objective of education of law is to cultivate legal awareness and empower individuals to exercise their rights and responsibilities effectively. This section explores the various methodologies employed in education of law, including interactive classroom instruction, experiential learning, mock trials, and community-based legal clinics. It also examines the integration of legal case studies, debates, and discussions into the curriculum, enabling students to analyze legal issues from different perspectives, develop critical thinking skills, and apply legal reasoning to real-world situations.

Education of law yields a wide range of outcomes and benefits for individuals and society at large. By acquiring legal literacy and understanding the principles of justice, citizens are better equipped to protect their rights, engage in informed decision-making, and participate actively in democratic processes. Furthermore, education of law promotes respect for the rule of law, enhances ethical awareness, and fosters a culture of legal compliance. It also contributes to the prevention of

---

12 A. Dudak, *The essence and importance of legal education*…op. cit, p. 72.
13 K. Economides, *Legal education*, [in:] *International encyclopedia of the social & behavioral sciences* (Second Edition), 2015, pp. 734–739.

legal disputes, the resolution of conflicts, and the establishment of a just and equitable society[14].

Integrating education of law into the broader educational curriculum is crucial to ensure that every individual receives the necessary legal knowledge and skills. This section examines the potential for incorporating education of law at various levels of education, including primary, secondary, and tertiary levels. It explores interdisciplinary approaches that connect law with other subjects, such as social studies, history, and ethics, fostering a holistic understanding of legal systems and their societal impact.

4. Basics of promoting legal education

Knowledge about the benefits of legal education must translate into the implementation of this form in the functioning of society. Civilizational changes force us to look for new educational solutions, enabling the best possible preparation of young generations for the changing world[15]. Although education is the exclusive competence of the Member States of the EU, this does not preclude the proposal and use of joint initiatives, programmes and various types of projects enabling social development[16].

In 2006, the European Parliament and the Council adopted a Recommendation on Key Competences for Lifelong Learning. It is defined as a combination of knowledge, skills and attitudes appropriate to the student's life, social and professional situation. It was recognized that in the era of current civilizational transformations they are necessary for personal self-fulfillment, being an active citizen, social cohesion and obtaining employment opportunities in the knowledge society[17]. Among the competences listed in the indicated document there are also social and civic competences, in which elements related to legal education can be found.

Social and civic competences are defined as competences covering the full range of behaviors that prepare individuals for effective and constructive participation in social and professional life, especially in increasingly diverse societies. They are intended to help prepare for full and active participation in civic life. The necessary knowledge, skills and attitudes related to this competence were m.in

14 S. S. Silbey, *Legal Culture and Legal* Consciousness, [in:] *International encyclopedia of the social & behavioral sciences* (Second Edition), 2015, pp. 726–733.

15 A. Syryt, *System kształcenia akademickiego prawników w Polsce wobec wymogów gospodarki opartej na wiedzy – rozważania na tle relacji między zasadami tworzenia programów studiów a normatywnymi kryteriami oceny jakości kształcenia,* „Krytyka Prawa" 2020, vol. 12, nr 2, pp. 120–121.

16 D. Dziewulak, *Edukacja prawna w szkolnictwie podstawowym i średnim w Polsce, wybranych państwach Unii Europejskiej oraz w Serbii i Wielkiej Brytanii,* „Zeszyty Prawnicze BAS" 2020, nr 4, pp. 220–221.

17 Recommendation of the European Parliament and of the Council of December 18, 2006 on Key Competences for Lifelong Learning (2006/962/EC).

understanding of the multicultural and socio-economic dimensions of European societies, as well as the mutual interaction of national cultural identity and European identity. Civic competence should be based on knowledge of the concepts of democracy, justice, equality, citizenship and citizens' rights and their application by different institutions at local, regional, national, European and international levels. They should be based on respect for human rights, including equality as the basis of democracy, and an understanding of the differences in the value systems of different religions and ethnic groups.

In 2018. The Council adopted a recommendation on key competences for lifelong learning[18]. The list and definitions of key competences have been modified and updated compared to the 2006 recommendations. The key competences include those related to civic competences. It should be stressed that the 2018 Recommendation also did not explicitly refer to legal education. Its elements can be found in civic competence, which is defined as the ability to act responsibly, civicly based on an understanding of social, economic, legal and political concepts and structures, as well as global events and sustainable development.

Civic competence is to be based on knowledge of basic concepts and phenomena concerning individuals, groups, professional organizations, society, economy and culture.

Raising awareness of the law and raising awareness requires the involvement of various actors, both public and social partners. Public entities, including public authorities, should create a systemic framework for legal education that would foster the development of society. The social partners, in particular professionals, should be involved in the promotion of law and raising legal awareness through dissemination and education activities[19].

5. Conclusions

In conclusion, education of law emerges as a pivotal component of civic education, enabling individuals to become informed, engaged, and responsible citizens. By equipping individuals with legal literacy and empowering them to exercise their rights and responsibilities, education of law fosters a culture of democracy, justice, and social cohesion. It is imperative for educational institutions, policymakers, and stakeholders to recognize the significance of education of law and integrate it into the educational curriculum to shape an educated citizenry capable of upholding the rule of law and actively participating in democratic processes.

---

18 Council Recommendation of 22 May 2018 on key competences for lifelong learning (2018/C 189/01).

19 A. S. Bartnik, *Poradnictwo prawne i obywatelskie w kontekście świadomości prawnej i potrzeby edukacji prawnej Polaków. Wybrane problemy*, „Studia Iuridica" 2019, no. 78, pp. 40–60.

In the doctrine, the term legal education is used to describe educational activities enabling the transfer of basic knowledge about the law to the public, in order to increase legal awareness. Through legal education, you can learn the principles of the functioning of the law and legal order, shape awareness of your rights and acquire respect for compliance with the law. The effectiveness of legal education depends on its universality and quality. Non-governmental organizations, local government institutions and government entities are important in this respect. Legal education can be implemented by disseminating knowledge about the law, presenting content on the Internet, trainings and courses, guides, textbooks and introducing legal topics to schools and universities.

The regulation of issues concerning legal education in normative acts concerning legal aid, the education system or the higher education system, and in particular the indication of standards for this form of education, is important for the development of awareness of the law and knowledge of the law in society. However, the formation of certain attitudes cannot be reduced to decreeing specific actions. Systemic actions for the dissemination of law and indicating its importance in the functioning of the state, society and economy are important.

Literature

Bartnik A. S., *Poradnictwo prawne i obywatelskie w kontekście świadomości prawnej i potrzeby edukacji prawnej Polaków. Wybrane problemy*, „Studia Iuridica" 2019, no. 78, pp. 40–60.

Boczek M., *Świadomość prawna Polaków wyzwaniem XXI wieku,* [in:] D. Gierszewski, H. A. Kretek (eds.), *Edukacja obywatelska dorosłych a społeczeństwo obywatelskie*, Racibórz 2015.

Czerepaniak-Walczak M., *Pedagogika emancypacyjna. Rozwój świadomości krytycznej człowieka*, Gdańsk 2006.

Dudak A., *Istota i znaczenie edukacji prawnej w kształtowaniu społeczeństwa otwartego*, „Przegląd Pedagogiczny" 2/2014.

Dziewulak D., *Edukacja prawna w szkolnictwie podstawowym i średnim w Polsce, wybranych państwach Unii Europejskiej oraz w Serbii i Wielkiej Brytanii*, „Zeszyty Prawnicze BAS" 2020, nr 4, pp. 220–221.

Economides K., *Legal Education,* [in:] J.D. Wright, *International encyclopedia of the social & behavioral sciences* (Second Edition), Elsevier, Amsterdam - Boston - Heidelberg - London - New York – Oxford - Paris - San Diego - San Francisco - Singapore - Sydney - Tokyo 2015.

Góralska R., Solarczyk-Szewc H., *O kompetencjach w kontekście Polskiej Ramy Kwalifikacji dla uczenia się przez całe życie*, „Edukacja Dorosłych" 2021, no. 2.

Klimski M., *Call for high quality education in the context of the postmodern society conception*, „Zeszyty Naukowe Politechniki Śląskiej. Seria: Organizacja i Zarządzanie" 2018, z. 122.

Kopińska V., *Edukacja prawna z perspektywy humanistyczno-krytycznej*, „Rocznik Andragogiczny“ 2012, vol. 19.

Silbey S. S., *Legal culture and legal* consciousness, [in:] J.D. Wright, *International encyclopedia of the social & behavioral sciences* (Second Edition), Elsevier, Amsterdam - Boston - Heidelberg - London - New York – Oxford - Paris - San Diego - San Francisco - Singapore - Sydney - Tokyo 2015.

Syryt A., *System kształcenia akademickiego prawników w Polsce wobec wymogów gospodarki opartej na wiedzy – rozważania na tle relacji między zasadami tworzenia programów studiów a normatywnymi kryteriami oceny jakości kształcenia*, „Krytyka Prawa“ 2020, vol. 12, nr 2.

Woźniakowska-Fajst D., *Edukacja prawna – możliwości, szanse, bariery*, Fundacja INPRIS, Warszawa 2012.

Marcin Klimski[1] and Katarzyna Uklańska[2]

Social aspects of legal education in the field of free legal aid: Challenges and opportunities from a sociological and pedagogical perspective

Abstract: The aim of the study is to formulate the postulates of effective legal education on the grounds of social sciences, one of the tasks of which is to disseminate knowledge about free legal aid. This will start with an analysis of the current legal status in the field of legal education; data from the control and monitoring of free legal aid and legal education system; phenomena of social exclusion.

Reports on the control and monitoring of the free legal aid system provide evidence that both the system and legal education are inadequate. In 2020, an amendment to the law on free legal aid and legal education was introduced, taking into account the recommendations contained in the reports. The question can be asked whether, in the new shape, the system is capable of providing effective legal education and will not exclude certain social categories.

In order to develop recommendations for effective legal education and avoid the dangers signaled, it is advisable to take advantage of the experience of sustainable education, aimed at, inter alia, shaping awareness of sustainable development, global goals, including those relating to education, social inclusion, and effective institutions.

Keywords: legal education, social exclusion, sustained learning

1. Introduction

The aim of the study is to formulate the postulates of effective legal education on the basis of social sciences as one of the tasks of which is to disseminate knowledge about free legal aid. The starting point will be the analysis of the current legal status in the field of legal education, data from the control of the free legal aid system and legal education, and the phenomenon of social exclusion. On the other

1 Cardinal Stefan Wyszyński University in Warsaw. ORCID: 0000-0002-9118-1673.
2 Cardinal Stefan Wyszyński University in Warsaw, ORCID: 00)0-0003-4477-7885.

hand, the model that will allow for the development of an appropriate model will be the experience of sustensive education, directed, inter alia, on shaping awareness of sustainable development, global goals, including those relating to education, social inclusion, and effective institutions.

Reports on the control and monitoring of the free legal aid system prove that both the system and the legal education introduced by the 2015 Act were ineffective. In 2018, the act was amended to include, inter alia, recommendations contained in the reports. It is worth asking yourself whether the new shape of the system is able to provide effective legal education and whether it will not exclude certain social categories?

The scope of the subject matter of this study and the specifics of the material, i.e., the existing normative acts as one of the sources, and the opinions of experts on the system of free legal aid, allow to use the experience of the well-known, but underestimated desk research method in sociology. It is based on the analysis of secondary material and belongs to the category of non-reactive research, i.e., research that does not affect the social behavior of the respondents[3]. The research uses existing materials, and it already takes place when reviewing the literature on the subject, which, however, may be only one of the sources of this method[4]. The analysis of existing data is either an initial stage of empirical research, or it can also be the basis for theoretical considerations[5]. For the purposes of this research, it will perform the latter function. In this case, the sources used will be the current legal regulations and the previous ones (as a presentation of the context for reports monitoring the operation of the system), concerning the system of free legal aid and legal education and reports on the control of the free legal aid system, as well as expert literature on the said system and education legal. This analysis will also take into account the literature on the phenomenon of social exclusion.

As for the part of the study that includes postulates to improve the effectiveness of legal education, it will be in the form of a recommendation. Recommendations will be formulated on the basis of good practices implemented within the framework of intensive education. The phenomenon of social exclusion is the subject of the global sustainable development goals set until 2030. Educational projects to counteract social exclusion relate to its digital and educational dimension but should also include the issues of legal exclusion.

Sociology as a science has cognitive functions, while its findings may have practical application[6]. When it comes to conscious use of the results of sociological

---

3 E. Babbie, *The practice of social research*, Belmont 2010 (12th edition), p. 332.

4 Z. Bednarowska, *Desk reserach – wykorzystanie potencjału danych zastanych w prowadzeniu badań marketingowych i społecznych*, „Marketing i rynek" 2015, no. 7, p. 18.

5 M. Makowska, R. Boguszewski, *Analiza danych zastanych – zagadnienia wstępne*, [w:] M. Makowska (ed.), *Analiza danych zastanych. Przewodnik dla studentów*, Warszawa 2013, p. 15.

6 S. Nowak, *Metody badań społecznych*, Warszawa 1985, pp. 448, 451.

research, and thus their practical use, they allow for the identification and diagnosis of specific social problems (understood here as a state of social reality deviating from what it should look like, a state perceived by the general public as threatening and in need of solution)[7]. Here, therefore, the researcher refers to specific values, sometimes basic ones, and, as a result, makes an assessment. Referring now to the issue that is the subject of this chapter – the formulation of postulates for effective legal education as one of the tasks of which is to disseminate knowledge about free legal aid – it should be emphasized that sociology is an adequate scientific discipline to identify problems important for the solutions of the current state of affairs.

In turn, the science of pedagogy in its operation is oriented towards issues related to the organization of the educational process, but also reflects on education that takes place in the perspective of the whole life. Hence the need for education, understood in a holistic perspective, to take into account the needs of a dynamically changing world. Emphasizing the problem of effective legal education, implemented, inter alia, in terms of free legal aid, it should be part of educational strategies and programs. Education is a process on the basis of which the subject acquires the knowledge necessary for proper functioning in the social reality. With the help of individual educational methods, it becomes possible to shape social awareness of specific problems, including access to free legal aid, which is not so obvious for representatives of all social groups, e.g., seniors.

Free legal services are the most common way for the state to protect citizens' access to the law[8]. J. Winczorek indicates two types of services of this type – free aid, as a private and individual activity, and free aid, more widespread, the cost of which is covered by a service provider or a third party, e.g., a state institution. This text will consider the latter type of free legal aid. The systems of this assistance are organized differently from country to country. In Poland, there is a system called judicare, where services are purchased on the market of independent service providers[9]. They also have a different subjective scope, i.e., different categories of people can use free services. The most frequently used access criterion is the income criterion.

---

7 See also K. Frysztacki, *Problemy społeczne*, [in] *Encyklopedia socjologii*, vol. 3, Warszawa 2000, pp. 205–208.

8 J. Winczorek, *Dostęp do prawa. Ujęcie socjologiczne*, Warszawa 2019, pp. 62–68.

9 Ibidem.

2. Legal education in the field of disseminating knowledge about access to free legal aid – implementation of statutory assumptions in the light of post-inspection results

The current legal status in the field of the system of free legal aid, free civic counseling and legal education is defined by the Free Legal Aid Act amended in 2018[10]. In 2021, changes were made to the law due to the SARS-CoV-2 virus pandemic[11]. However, this did not change the fundamental core of the law. Apart from the principles of free legal aid, the document is also a way to increase the legal awareness of the society. From 1 January 2019, legal education services are provided by non-governmental entities under an appropriate agreement for running a counseling center. As part of legal education, society is sensitized to the issues of civic rights and obligations, the functioning of domestic and foreign legal protection authorities, mediation and methods of amicable settlement of disputes, the possibility of citizens participating in public consultations in the field of law-making, access to free civic counseling and free legal aid[12]. Legal education, addressed to adults, is a kind of protection that helps to prevent the phenomenon of social exclusion. It often happens that the elderly do not benefit from this form of counseling because they are not aware of their rights in this regard. The interested parties who want to take advantage of this form of education mainly depend on a properly functioning system of legal information. It is about the possibility of reliable and efficient obtaining of knowledge about the reported problem, as well as obtaining legal advice from competent persons[13].

During the year in which the law on free legal aid and legal education came into force (2016), many of its non-functionalities and ineffectiveness in the planned system were observed. These irregularities were noticed already in 2016, thanks to the monitoring of the free legal aid system carried out by the Institute of Public Affairs (ISP) and the Polish American Freedom Foundation (PAFF), as well as during an audit, the results of which were published in 2018 by the Supreme Audit Office

10 Act of 15 June 2018 amending the Free Legal Aid Act. The amendment introduces the term civic counseling, and its new title reads: "The Act on free legal aid, free civic counseling and legal education".

11 A. Dudak, *Istota i znaczenie edukacji prawnej w kształtowaniu społeczeństwa obywatelskiego*, „Przegląd Pedagogiczny" 2014, no. 2, p. 70.

12 https://darmowapomocprawna.ms.gov.pl/pl/edukacja-prawna/ (accessed: 27.02.2021).

13 *Funkcjonowanie systemu nieodpłatnej pomocy. Informacja o wynikach kontroli*, LOP 430.001.2018 registration number 4/2018 / P / 17/090 / LOP, p. 21, https://www.nik.gov.pl/kontrole/P/17/090/ (accessed: 11.01.2021); Instytut Spraw Publicznych (ISP), Polsko-Amerykańska Fundacja Wolności (PAFW), *Raport końcowy z monitoringu funkcjonowania nieodpłatnej pomocy prawnej*, Warszawa 2016, pp. 3–4, https://www.gov.pl/web/sprawiedliwosc/edukacja-prawna2, (accessed: 13.11.2023).

(NIK). The results of these analyzes will be presented, in particular, however, in the area of legal education in the field of free legal aid[14]. Civic counseling, on the other hand, was not introduced to the act at the time.

Both audits, although using different methods of verifying the effects of the introduced system and the obligation of legal education, indicated similar irregularities[15]. Attention was drawn to the shortcomings of the system, such as: on the fact that: it was planned ineffectively in financial terms, the beneficiaries were defined too narrowly (the homeless, disabled, self-employed, unemployed, single-parents were not included), acted mainly in the field of legal information, not legal counseling, did not use the possibilities of non-governmental organizations, The information campaign about the system was also poorly planned and it was directed to the wrong social category – few people benefited from the help, which resulted from the ignorance of such a possibility (0.7 % in January and 1.2 % in November according to CBOS and every hundredth Pole according to data of the Ministry of Justice). The representatives of social organizations and the Council of Free Legal Aid at the Minister of Justice also pointed to the poor promotion of information on access points to free legal aid.

The comment regarding the information campaign is related to the element of the system – legal education. The reports emphasized that this education, as a duty of public administration bodies to increase the legal awareness of citizens, was not specified in any way in the act. The system also does not provide financial resources for information activities and legal education[16]. The provisions of the Act of 2015 "do not grant the above-mentioned bodies with additional competences, do not specify the method of carrying out educational activities, and do not allocate separate funds for their implementation"[17]. It is indicated that the activities to increase awareness of free legal aid were carried out by: the website maintained by the Ministry of Justice (Ministry of Justice) (www.darmowapomocprawna.ms.gov.pl), a request of the Ministry of Justice to the presidents of courts of appeal to standardize information on websites individual courts regarding the above-mentioned assistance, state media campaign conducted in 2015 and written responses of the Ministry of Justice regarding the interpretation and application of the applicable provisions on free legal aid and publishing them on websites[18]. The Ministry also undertook other educational activities, such as the continuation of the project under the National Development Strategy until 2020, one of the activities of which was aimed at broadening the public's access to legal information and legal services. The project School education against legal exclusion was also implemented,

14 ISP, PAFW, *Raport końcowy...*, p. 5.
15 *Funkcjonowanie systemu nieodpłatnej pomocy...*, p. 53.
16 Ibidem, pp. 54–55.
17 https://www.gov.pl/web/sprawiedliwosc/edukacja-prawna2, https://www.gov.pl/web/sprawiedliwosc/edukacja-prawna2 (accessed: 10.02.2021).
18 *Funkcjonowanie systemu nieodpłatnej pomocy...*, p. 56.

the aim of which was to increase access to the knowledge of the most vulnerable, e.g., minorities (workshops were conducted in lower secondary and upper secondary schools all over Poland). Moreover, an educational and legal guide was created, dedicated to children and adolescents over 12 years of age (A student comes to a lawyer). These projects have led to the creation of websites on legal education and mediation[19]. The Ministry of Justice also organized conferences on this subject, and on its website, in the Legal Education tab, it placed information related to this issue.

The described activities of the Ministry of Justice for the benefit of legal education are assessed by the Supreme Audit Office as insufficient and not being elements of a uniform strategy[20]. It was noted that they were uneven (many, various forms addressed to students, and not much to other social categories) and not adapted to the capabilities of those who could benefit from such help (information posted mainly on the Internet, which eliminates digitally excluded people). This is related to the conclusion formulated earlier in the PSI report that only 3 % of interested persons used the services of the system, and those who did not use the system's services to a large extent, indicated their ignorance as to the existence of such a possibility as the main reason[21]. Then, in 2018, the INPRIS Foundation carried out a survey on the brand awareness of the free legal aid system. It confirmed that the main reason the respondents did not use the advice was their ignorance of the existence of such a possibility[22].

The functioning of the act in practice has been widely criticized. Various bodies formulated postulates for changes[23]. The results of the inspections also resulted in recommendations regarding the repair of the system. In the field of legal education, it was postulated that the tasks included in it should be defined and the methods of their implementation and financing should be indicated[24]. An indirect reference was made to legal education, requesting the separation of legal information and advice and making legal information a publicly available service. It also indicated the need to include in the subsidies awarded for running points, the costs of activities related to information about the activities of these points and verification of the quality of services provided[25]. The necessity to introduce civic

---

19 ISP, PAFW, *Raport końcowy...*, op. cit., pp. 3–4.

20 J. Winczorek, *Dostęp do...*, p. 281.

21 F. Czernicki, J. Winczorek, *Stanowisko przedstawicieli...*, https://ofop.eu/stanowisko-przedstawicieli-organizacji-spolecznych-czlonkow-rady-nieodplatnej-pomocy-prawnej-i-edukacji-prawnej-przy-ms-w-sprawie-podsumowania-roku-funkcjonowania-i-koniecznych-zmian-w-ustawie-o-nieo/ (accessed: 13.11.2023).

22 ISP, PAFW, *Raport końcowy...*, op. cit., p. 6.

23 Ibidem, pp. 5–6.

24 *Funkcjonowanie systemu nieodpłatnej pomocy. ...*, p. 62; J. Winczorek, *Dostęp do...*, pp. 278–281.

25 T. Kowalak, *Marginalność i marginalizacja społeczna*, Warszawa 1998, p. 31.

counseling to the act was pointed out. The system was considered ineffective and in need of changes, although necessary[26].

3. Educational, legal and digital exclusion – barriers to legal education in disseminating knowledge about free legal aid

Taking into account the conclusions and recommendations described above, there are several difficulties related to legal education in the area of access to free legal aid. They also determine the causes of system failure. You can try to describe them using the concept of social exclusion – for the purposes of this chapter, it is necessary to analyze the barriers that have appeared in the way of effective legal education in the field of free legal aid, referring to educational, legal and digital exclusion. It was indicated in the post-inspection reports that the planned system did not take into account digitally excluded groups and those most in need of free legal aid. They are often people with lower competences and qualifications, operating outside the center of social life, without high income. These categories may or may not overlap, resulting in an unsatisfactory level of use of free legal services.

In social sciences, trying to define the situation of limited access to various social opportunities, the concept of social exclusion is used. Persons or groups are subject to social exclusion as exclusions from social structures[27]. It is reducing access to the conditions and way of life commonly accepted in a given community. It is also a state of deprivation of basic social needs and an unsatisfactory place in society[28]. Social exclusion is defined in terms of a process during which individual limitations may accumulate and the beginning of the road to social exclusion may be e.g., job loss[29]. It also indicates specific social categories that are exposed to exclusion, e.g., unemployed people, children and young people from disadvantaged backgrounds, women outside the labor market, people with low qualifications[30]. This pathological social phenomenon has many dimensions. Restrictions on the access of individuals and groups are observed e.g., on the level of education, economics, politics or new communication technologies, as well as law.

One of the dimensions of this exclusion is educational exclusion, which consists in "inability to participate in important aspects of collective life: social, economic or political, resulting from a low level of education. Marginalization in the area of education can also be defined in terms of discrimination and refer to inequalities

---

26 A. Belcer, *Zbędni, odtrąceni i niechciani – wykluczeni!,* [in:] M. Pokrzywa (ed.), *Wykluczenie społeczne. Diagnoza, wymiarI i kierunadandań*, S. Wilk, p. 10.

27 Ibidem, p. 12.

28 Ibidem, p. 11.

29 J. Włodarczyk, N. Gańko, *Wykluczenie edukacyjne*, „Dzieci się liczą", 2011, no. 3, p. 61.

30 P. Żuk, *O nierównościach edukacyjnych w Polsce*, [in:] P. Żuk (ed.), *Podziały klasowe i nierówności społeczne*, Warszawa 2010, pp. 217, 221.

in access to education and broadly understood culture"[31]. Educational inequalities in Poland are still strong, despite universal access to the education system. It is clear that social origin affects the possibility of acquiring knowledge and education, and the factors that co-determine the education of children are the education of parents, place of residence and the level of education of the environment they come from[32]. The educational system also does not support the weakest students. The latter therefore remain at the bottom of the educational career ladder and complete the biblical parable of the talents[33]. Developing a knowledge society is the minimum necessary to be able to function in its structures, it determines life chances and social positions[34].

Legal exclusion, as A. Kojder writes, although it objectively exists, does not take the form of orders, prohibitions or behaviors; exists as "a certain legal and social context"[35]. He determines the legal position of the addressees of statutory law. J. Winczorek defines legal exclusion as "the inability to participate in communication in the legal system. A person deprived of access to the law for lack of the necessary resources, knowledge, cultural competence, organization or time is eliminated from this communication"[36]. It is indicated that the legal amendments support those parts of society that already have capital, those that are privileged and have power[37]. There is a secondary social victimization here, because legal exclusion is related to the financial and cultural capital of an individual[38].

Despite the widespread access to the Internet[39], everyday life in the company of new technologies, the phenomenon of digital exclusion is observed. People who do not take advantage of these types of opportunities are socially excluded. The digital divide refers to "the difference between those who have regular access to digital and information technologies and are able to use it effectively, and those who do not"[40]. These differences affect people's life chances, their labor market

---

31 M. Zahorska, *Edukacja drogą marginalizacji?*, [in:] K. Slany, Z. Seręga (eds.), *Sprostać zmianom. Szkice o powinnościach współczesnej socjologii*, Kraków 2009, p. 196.
32 P. Długosz, *Wykluczenie edukacyjne wśród młodzieży – przypadek gimnazjalistów z południa Polski*, [in:] M. Pokrzywa, S. Wilk (eds.), *Wykluczenie społeczne. Diagnoza, wymiary i kierunki badań*, p. 154.
33 A. Kojder, *Podstawy socjologii prawa*, Warszawa 2016, p. 295.
34 J. Winczorek, *Dostęp do…*, op. cit., p. 346.
35 A. Bartnik, K. J. Kowalska, *Nieodpłatna pomoc prawna*, Warszawa 2019, p. 34.
36 A. Turska, *Prawo i wykluczenie. Studium empiryczne*, Warszawa 2010.
37 See: *Korzystanie z Internetu.* Communication from CBOS research No. 85/2020, p. 4 https://www.cbos.pl/SPISKOM.POL/2020/K_085_20.PDF, (accessed: 22.02.2021).
38 D. Batorski, *Wykluczenie cyfrowe w Polsce*, „Studia BAS" 2009, no. 3, p. 225.
39 W. Tyburski, *Wprowadzenie*, [in:] W. Tyburski (ed.), *Zasady kształtowania postaw sprzyjających wdrażaniu zrównoważonego rozwoju*, Toruń 2011, p. 7.
40 *Transforming our world: the 2030 Agenda for Sustainable Development.* Resolution adopted by the General Assembly on 25 September 2015.

situation and opportunities to participate in social and cultural life. They affect physical access to digital media and competences in using them.

The aforementioned types of social exclusion are realized in the case of people to whom free legal aid is dedicated. They are excluded from knowledge about this system due to various circumstances characteristic of educational, legal and digital exclusion.

4. Good educational practices as an opportunity to improve the system of free legal aid

Social exclusion in all its forms is a global phenomenon that is closely related to the issue of sustainable development. The implementation of the assumptions of sustainable development is an international response to the current development model that threatens human well-being and harms its further existence. In this way, the aim is to implement a new vision of development postulating "(...) thinking that decisively corrects the current nature of our relations with the world of nature, social and economic life"[41]. The direction of changes is shown in the 2030 Agenda for Sustainable Development, which includes 17 Sustainable Development Goals[42]. Some of them are related to the issue of social exclusion, and their consistent implementation helps to eliminate this phenomenon and thus improve the quality of people's lives. In order to be able to improve the quality of the provision of free legal aid services, it is worth intensifying activities towards the so-called "Good practices". Commonly understood, these are activities that result in a specific positive outcome. Good practices are activities that are characterized by the implementation of innovative solutions, can be implemented in other areas of the educational process and, importantly, are repeatable and can be applied by interested persons or institutions. These are, for example, suggestions on how to properly respond to perceived irregularities and solve problematic situations. It seems that a helpful issue in the field of legal education, which already works well in intensive education, is focusing on local activities. Therefore, entities dealing with solving social problems in the field of legal education and free legal aid have new challenges related to the need to change existing activities, which were primarily aimed at helping those who needed it. The practice of intensive education shows that the model of active social policy works well, in which the growing importance of local self-government, empowering local communities and voluntary activities is emphasized. Non-governmental organizations are of great importance; therefore, they should be allowed to participate in the implementation of public tasks as a key – and in the areas of educational policy the most important – partner of

41 D. Bednarczyk, *Przeciwdziałanie wykluczeniu cyfrowemu (e-integracja) w Polsce*, „Biuletyn EBIB" 2014, no. 9, p. 2.

42 B. Kołaczek, *Dostęp młodzieży do edukacji. Zróżnicowania, uwarunkowania, wyrównywanie szans*, Warszawa 2004, p. 16.

local government. In the model of approach to solving social problems, including the phenomenon of exclusion, adopted in intensive education, there is a practice which focuses on local activities that also take into account the participation of citizens themselves. It is the creation of "help for self-help" mechanisms, under which good practices are extended also by people who have previously been affected by, for example, the problem of digital exclusion. The idea is that, for example, counteracting digital exclusion, which translates into access to information, including information on free legal aid, should not only focus on large cities, but also reach smaller communities. The restriction of access to digital information is subject to a certain gradation. The first stage, also known as the hard barrier, is the physical and material ability to enjoy technological benefits. It is about the inability to purchase specific equipment. The second level, classified as soft barriers, concerns psychological and competence issues. This type of digital exclusion exposes the lack of knowledge, skills and competences to be able to use educational tools such as computers, smartphones, the Internet[43]. In order to overcome both hard and soft barriers, legal education programs should be supported by local initiatives to promote them, on the one hand, and, on the other hand, to actually reach people in need, offering them specific help.

5. Conclusions

The knowledge that is gained in the process of education and training gives competences, professional efficiency, but also shapes human consciousness, allows him to understand the world, develop feelings and values and thus lead himself[44].

As noted by G. Skąpska, effective communication on the subject of law influences the shaping of legal awareness of the recipients of the information provided[45]. On the one hand, it is understood as the one whose effect is the understanding and assimilation of the content of the law by the recipients, and then compliance with it[46]. On the other hand, it is communication which results in creating positive associations with the legal system and creating trust in it. Popular culture and the mass media are of great importance for such effective communication on the subject of law. Television series, including criminal ones or the popular press, can help in shaping legal knowledge and attitude to the law[45]. Of course, these are just some suggestions that can be included in the so-called methods of effective legal education. In order to indicate good educational practices in the field of sensitizing the society to the possibility of reaching for free legal aid, it is worth taking

43 G. Skapska, *Komunikacja o prawie a świadomość i kultura prawna – krótki komentarz socjologa*, [in:] *Sprostać zmianom. Szkice o powinnościach współczesnej socjologii*, Kraków 2009, p. 249.

44 Ibidem, p. 247.

45 Ibidem, p. 249.

46 M. J. Szymański, *Edukacyjne problemy współczesności*, Kraków 2014, pp. 34–35.

into account the proven methods used by sustensive education. Its content focuses on global issues included in the 2030 Agenda for Sustainable Development. The problems indicated by the 17 Sustainable Development Goals are largely oriented towards counteracting the phenomenon of social exclusion taking place in various aspects of social life. "More and more is being said about the danger of widening the scale of marginalization and exclusion of a significant part of the population, condemned to an existence that has little to do with the level and development trends of modern society"[46]. The dynamics of the signaled social exclusions include, inter alia, on the fact that we are dealing with an aging society that functions in a digitized environment. Not every senior citizen, or a person with even a slight disability, is able to cope with this reality without the help of others. The ability to search for information on the Internet becomes a barrier to using free legal aid. This also translates into the effectiveness of informing about free legal aid, which was pointed out by the authors of the post-inspection reports.

The issues that are the subject of intensive education are conveyed to recipients based on various methods. In addition to those that are implemented in the so-called "School bench" and take place during formal education, also those in the informal area are used. The second form of education, firstly, is carried out, inter alia, by various non-governmental entities, and secondly, it is extended throughout life, which allows, for example, seniors to become the subject of such educational activities. Therefore, in order to be able to talk about effective legal education in the field of disseminating knowledge about free legal aid, it is worth:

- to provide information about it in an appropriate form to the entities of the educational process, especially those who face certain limitations;
- for people with different socio-economic status to have access to it, as there is still a belief in the public awareness that all legal services are paid;
- focusing on local activities conducted by non-governmental institutions, promoting volunteering and media initiatives in this area.

The postulate of providing good-quality education in the context of free legal aid is extremely timely. Knowledge in the field of law should be realized in educational systems that can be successfully implemented based on the experience of sustensive education. The perceived problems of the globalizing world, included in the Sustainable Development Goals, define the effects of the actions of society, often focused on the fulfillment of "here and now".

Literature

Babbie E., *The Practice of Social Research*, Belmont 2010 (12th edition).

Bartnik A., Kowalska K. J., *Nieodpłatna pomoc prawna*, Warszawa 2019.

Batorski D., *Wykluczenie cyfrowe w Polsce*, „Studia BAS“ 2009, no. 3.

Bednarczyk D., *Przeciwdziałanie wykluczeniu cyfrowemu (e-integracja) w Polsce*, „Biuletyn EBIB“ 2014, no. 9.

Bednarowska Z., *Desk reserach – wykorzystanie potencjału danych zastanych w prowadzeniu badań marketingowych i społecznych*, „Marketing i rynek" 2015, no. 7.

Belcer A., *Zbędni, odtrąceni i niechciani – wykluczeni!*, [in:] M. Pokrzywa, S. Wilk (eds.), *Wykluczenie społeczne. Diagnoza, wymiary i kierunki badań*, Rzeszów 2013.

Czernicki F., Winczorek J., *Stanowisko przedstawicieli organizacji społecznych, członków Rady Nieodpłatnej Pomocy Prawnej i Edukacji Prawnej przy Ministrze Sprawiedliwości w sprawie podsumowania roku funkcjonowania i koniecznych zmian w ustawie o nieodpłatnej pomocy prawnej i edukacji prawnej*, https://publicystyka.ngo.pl/nieodplatna-pomoc-prawna-po-roku-stanowisko-organizacji, [accessed: 09.02.2021].

Długosz P., *Wykluczenie edukacyjne wśród młodzieży – przypadek gimnazjalistów z południa Polski*, [in:] M. Pokrzywa, S. Wilk (eds.), *Wykluczenie społeczne. Diagnoza, wymiary i kierunki badań*, Rzeszów 2013.

Dudak A., *Istota i znaczenie edukacji prawnej w kształtowaniu społeczeństwa obywatelskiego*, „Przegląd Pedagogiczny" 2014, no. 2.

Frysztacki K., *Problemy społeczne*, [in:] *Encyklopedia socjologii*, t. 3, Warszawa 2008.

Funkcjonowanie systemu nieodpłatnej pomocy. Informacja o wynikach kontroli, LOP 430.001.2018 no ewid.4/2018/P/17/090/LOP, s. 21, https://www.nik.gov.pl/kontrole/P/17/090/ [accessed: 11.01.2021].

Instytut Spraw Publicznych, Polsko-Amerykańska Fundacja Wolności, *Raport końcowy z monitoringu funkcjonowanianieodpłatnejpomocyprawnej*, Warszawa 2016, https://www.isp.org.pl/pl/publikacje/raport-koncowy-z-monitoringu-funkcjonowania-systemu-nieodplatnej-pomocy-prawnej, [accessed: 11.01.2021].

Kojder A., *Podstawy socjologii prawa*, Warszawa 2016.

Kołaczek B., *Dostęp młodzieży do edukacji. Zróżnicowania, uwarunkowania, wyrównywanie szans*, Warszawa 2004.

Korzystanie z Internetu. Komunikat z badań CBOS no 85/2020, p. 4, https://www.cbos.pl/SPISKOM.POL/2020/K_085_20.PDF, [accessed: 22.02.2021].

Kowalak T., *Marginalność i marginalizacja społeczna*, Warszawa 1998.

Makowska M., Boguszewski R., *Analiza danych zastanych – zagadnienia wstępne*, [in:] M. Makowska (ed.), *Analiza danych zastanych. Przewodnik dla studentów*, Warszawa 2013.

Nowak S., *Metody badań społecznych*, Warszawa 1985.

Skapska G., *Komunikacja o prawie a świadomość i kultura prawna – krótki komentarz socjologa*, [in:] K. Slany, Z. Seręga (eds.), *Sprostać zmianom. Szkice o powinnościach współczesnej socjologii*, Kraków 2009.

Szymański M.J., *Edukacyjne problemy współczesności*, Kraków 2014.

Transforming our world: The 2030 Agenda for Sustainable Development. Resolution adopted by the General Assembly on 25 September 2015.

Turska A., *Prawo i wykluczenie. Studium empiryczne,* Warszawa 2010.

Tyburski W., *Wprowadzenie,* [in:] W. Tyburski (ed.), *Zasady kształtowania postaw sprzyjającychwdrażaniu zrównoważonego rozwoju,* Toruń 2011.

Winczorek J., *Dostęp do prawa. Ujęcie socjologiczne,* Warszawa 2019.

Włodarczyk J., Gańko N., *Wykluczenie edukacyjne,* „Dzieci się liczą", 2011, no 3.

Zahorska M., *Edukacja drogą marginalizacji?,* [in:] K. Slany, Z. Seręga (eds.), *Sprostać zmianom. Szkice o powinnościach współczesnej socjologii,* Warszawa 2009.

Żuk P., *O nierównościach edukacyjnych w Polsce,* [in:] P. Żuk (ed.), *Podziały klasowe i nierówności społeczne,* Warszawa 2010.

Kazimiera Juszka[1] and Karolina Głowacka[2]

University legal information clinics in the free of charge legal aid system

Abstract: University legal information clinics have been playing a crucial role in providing legal aid and education in Poland for over 20 years. The chapter examines the principles and features of university legal information clinics, including their reliance on reliability, administrative and substantive supervision, provision of free services, use of written form, and confidentiality. The chapter also discusses the subjective and objective scope of these clinics, highlighting their wider access to information and legal advice for individuals excluded from the traditional free legal aid system. It further examines the problems faced by university legal information clinics, such as financial constraints, insufficient support, barriers in reaching clients, lack of professional secrecy, and institutional obstacles. The chapter concludes by emphasizing the importance of university legal information clinics in addressing social issues and providing practical legal education.

Keywords: University legal information clinics, legal education, free legal aid, access to justice, legal clinics

1. Introduction

University legal information clinics in Poland have been operating for over 20 years, the first one being Jagiellonian University Student Legal Information Clinic, established in 1997. In the 2018/2019 academic year, there were 27 university legal information clinics located in 17 cities[3]. The number of clinics is constantly growing, and this is mainly due to the creation of new departments and

---

1 University of National Education Commission in Cracow. ORCID: 0000-0002-8466-1716.

2 University of the National Education Commission in Krakow. ORCID: 0000-0002-7422-992X.

3 Foundation of University Legal Information Clinics, *Annual report on the activities of the clinics in the 2018/2019 academic year of 5 February 2020* Electronic access: http://www.fupp.org.pl/co-nowego/9-polski/aktualnosci/295-roczne-sprawozdanie-z-dzialalnosci-poradni-w-roku-akademickim-2018-2019 (accessed: 10.12.2020).

faculties of law at successive universities. An example is the Student Legal Information Clinic operating since 2018 as part of the Faculty of Law and Economics of the Pedagogical University.

2. Principles of operation for university legal information clinics

A student legal information clinic is a type of legal aid organization which provides legal aid and assistance to poor persons in the community, and, at the same time, supplies machinery in a law school by which students may, under proper supervision, learn certain specific things about the actual practice of law[4]. The above definition, although it was formulated almost a hundred years ago, fully reflects the essence of the law information clinic, emphasizing two basic and complementary objectives of its functioning. The first one, supplementing the existing theoretical model of education, provides law students with a chance to develop practical skills, and due to its educational value, it seems to be of paramount importance. The second, more important and socially significant objective, is to provide free legal aid to persons who are unable to cover the costs of the fees of a legal adviser or attorney[5]. In their activities, university legal information clinics follow the principles of:

1. reliability, which is manifested in, inter alia, by training in the ethics of legal professions and principles of conducting conversations with clients, as well as seminars devoted to discussing given cases;
2. administrative and substantive supervision, exercised by the teaching and research staff as well as attorneys and legal advisers;
3. being free of charge;
4. using written form within the information obligation on the principles of providing aid by the clinic and providing legal advice in writing;
5. confidentiality assuring the security of documents and clients' personal data.

University clinics had not been included in the free legal aid system by the Free Legal Aid Act nor subsequent amendments. The above decision was justified by different objectives of operation of the student counseling clinics being different from the assumptions and objectives of the free legal counseling system. It was indicated that the primary goal of counseling clinics, operating within the

---

4 J. S. Bradway, *The nature of a legal aid clinic*, Southern California Law Review 1930, Vol. III, p. 173.

5 Cf. M. Szewczyk, *Idea uniwersyteckich poradni prawnych*, Clinic 1999, No. 1, p. 14. J. S. Bradway, *The legal aid clinic: A means of building tough mental fiber*, Southern California Law Review 1931, Vol. V, p. 36. M. A. Du Plessis, *Clinical legal education: Determining the mission and focus of a university law clinic and required outcomes, skills & values*, De Jure 2015, Vol. 48, No. 2, p. 313.

organizational framework of law faculties, is to educate students. On the other hand, the main objective of the Act is to provide legal advice at the highest level, which is possible by entrusting the provision of this aid to attorneys and legal advisers[6]. The Ombudsman intervened in this regard, addressing the Minister of Justice in 2015, and the President of the Republic of Poland two years later. The Ombudsman noted that law clinics have experience in providing free legal counseling, the work of students is supervised by academic teachers, legal advisers and attorneys, and legal opinions prepared by the clinics are detailed, exhaustive and on high substantive level[7].

3. Subjective scope

Paradoxically, the fact that student information legal clinics were not included in the system of free legal aid contributed to providing the society with wider access to information and legal advice. In the years 2016–2019, universities were not limited by the subjective scope of the Act in its original wording. Students had the opportunity to provide legal aid to people who cannot afford it, who were refused free legal advice under the system due to failure to meet restrictive conditions. The limits adopted in the Act excluded social groups whose financial situation made it impossible to take advantage of paid legal advice but was too "good" to allow them to receive social aid benefits. The catalogue of beneficiaries did not include people with disabilities and serious illnesses, recipients of annuity benefits, single parents, people suffering from domestic violence, unemployed and homeless, foreigners, crime victims and prison inmates.

4. Objective scope

Cases related to civil law prevail among the activities of student legal information clinics, as in the system of advice provided by attorneys and legal advisers. In the case of university clinics, there cases concerned primarily the analysis of the provisions of civil law contracts, the preparation of pleadings during proceedings (lawsuits, appeals, applications to reinstate the timetable for the proceedings, objections), consumer law, compensation and redress, inheritance law. Criminal cases accounted for a higher percentage of all cases received in student legal information clinics than in the public system. Students, inter alia, prepared pleadings during proceedings (notices about committing a crime, appeals, applications for an aggregate sentence, complaints about prolixity, subsidiary, and private indictments), and provided information on electronic supervision, consequences of voluntary submission to punishment, rules of interrogation. In the field of family law, university legal information clinics prepared, among others, divorce

---

6 Letter of the Minister of Justice of 19 June 2015, ref. DL-VII-4670-18/15.
7 Letter of the Ombudsman to the President of 6th July 2017, ref. RP IV.510.9.2014.AB.

and separation petitions, as well as petitions for incapacitation, establishment, limitation, withdrawal of parental authority, informed about the grounds for alimony and obliged persons. Among the cases dealt with by students of university legal information clinics, there were also cases in the field of housing and cooperative law (concerning eviction, substitute housing, social, communal and occasional rental), tax matters (tax obligations, entitlement to reliefs, overpayments, corrections, liability for tax arrears, preparation of applications for individual tax interpretations), in the field of law and administrative proceedings (appeals to higher instance authorities, the Provincial Administrative Court, the Supreme Administrative Court, the Self-government Appeal Court, drafting complaints about the inactivity of the authority, matters related to the rights of refugees and foreigners – legalization of stay, Pole's Card, granting Polish citizenship), as well as many other cases related to the occurrence of students in disciplinary proceedings at universities, animal law, economic law and issues related to the constitutional complaint and complaint to the ECtHR[8].

In the objective scope of university legal information clinics and the system of free legal counseling, the most important difference seems to be the procedural stage. In the Act of 2015, a narrow catalogue has been drawn up which does not include the preparation of pleadings and providing advice in pending proceedings. The Ombudsman also drew attention to this issue, formalized court procedures constitute the greatest obstacle to pursuing rights, and the real problem is, for example, understanding and remembering the instruction given orally at the hearing on the methods of lodging means of challenge or the correct calculation of procedural time limits. It can be concluded that student legal information clinics supplement the system of free legal counseling with aspects that are not provided for by the Act, until 2019 in the subjective or objective scope.

5. Problems related to the functioning of university legal information clinics

According to the data of the Ministry of Justice, the number of legal advices provided as part of free legal aid has been increasing year by year[9], this proves the system is popular. However, there are still cases when people seeking free legal aid

8 Annual report on the activities of the clinics in the 2018/2019 academic year published by the University Legal Clinics Foundation on 5 February 2020.

9 *The number of consultations increases each year: in 2018, 452 584 consultations were provided, and in 2019 there were 455 055 of them in total. The number of beneficiaries is also increasing, in 2018 there were 385 387 of them and in 2019 as many as 437 895 people. This gives an increase in 2019 by as much as 13.62 percent, as compared to the previous year, electronic access:* https://samorzad.pap.pl/kategoria/aktualnosci/ms-stopniowo-wracaja-w-formie-stacjonarnej-punkty-bezplatnej-pomocy-prawnej (accessed: 10.12.2020).

go to law firms run by professional attorneys. According to the research conducted using the diagnostic survey method in the period from September 2018 to December 2019 (16 months), 73 persons contacted one of the law firms in Krakow (by phone or in person) expecting to receive free legal advice. Every month, an average of 4–5 people came to one law firm but considering that some legal firms operating on the market encounter such events, the scale of the phenomenon may be much larger. Questions mainly concerned civil law in a broad sense (inheritance, property, family, and consumer law), as well as criminal, administrative, labor, and social security law. The reason why persons entitle to receive free legal advice came to entities conducting paid activities was mostly (over 50 %) lack of awareness of the existence of a free legal counseling system and university legal information clinics. The second most frequent reason was the inability to obtain telephone advice (less than 29 % of the total number of respondents, and 44 % of people calling the law firm), fears resulting from the very low legal awareness of the beneficiaries (e.g., some people were not aware of the amendment to the subjective scope of the Act, e.g., no age restrictions, two persons believed that legal advisers cannot provide aid in criminal cases; three people raised concerns about the impartiality of attorneys and legal advisers providing advice at the seats of offices, objections were also raised as to the quality of free services, excessive bureaucracy, inconvenient locations and working hours of the clinic).

The above data on the level of legal awareness of the beneficiaries correspond to the results presented by the Supreme Audit Office as part of the audit carried out in 2018[10]. Persons providing free legal advice assessed that the legal awareness of almost 85 % of clients was insufficient or extremely low. In this context, the issue of legal education appears to be urgent, and the legislator has granted the possibility of implementing tasks in this area to, inter alia, universities offering higher education in the field of law, and therefore also to university legal information clinics.

Acting long before the creation of the public system of free legal aid, student legal information clinics became an important factor in the fight against social exclusion, providing a substitute for equal access to information and legal advice, even though their activities were, and still are, significantly limited for financial, logistic and location reasons. The most frequently indicated problems by student legal information clinics included insufficient financial resources (preventing the organization of more training courses, seminars and conferences, maintenance and improvement of technical equipment, specialist literature, licenses and secure databases), insufficient support from universities and the legal community (in terms of increasing the staff, the possibility of consultation and cooperation with other faculties/departments, referring eligible clients to the clinic), barriers in reaching the clients (e.g. the problem of digital exclusion of some beneficiaries,

---

10 Supreme Audit Office, *Funkcjonowanie systemu nieodpłatnej pomocy prawnej*, ref. no. LOP 430.001.2018, no. 4/2018/P/17/090. Electronic access: https://www.nik.gov.pl/kontrole/P/17/090/ (accessed: 10.12.2020).

too weak marketing activities), no professional secrecy (internal regulations oblige students to keep secrecy, but there is no legal instrument for securing secrecy before the courts; in practice, there were cases when a student accompanying a client at a hearing was spontaneously summoned to testify as a witness[11]. In such a situation, the student, unlike an attorney or legal adviser, cannot refuse to answer questions), institutional barriers (no legal and systemic framework for the clinic's activities, no forms of cooperation between the clinic and the administration and judiciary).

On the other hand, the shortcomings most often indicated by clients of student legal information clinics or, more broadly, free legal counseling, was insufficient attention and time given by persons giving advice, providing information in a language incomprehensible to clients, the inability to obtain advice by phone, too much bureaucracy, inconvenient locations and office hours of the clinic[12].

6. Conclusions

As already indicated, university legal information clinics not only help to cope with social problems affecting especially the most disadvantaged people but are also an important element of education. It should be noted that the role of universities is primarily to impart theoretical knowledge, but universities are increasingly trying to provide elements of practical professional education in the curricula of law studies, which should be considered a positive phenomenon. The field of law with a practical profile at the Pedagogical University reflects the above. Social changes make it necessary to adjust the operation of the free legal aid system and university legal information clinics to the needs of the beneficiaries. The recent amendment to the Act in question exemplifies a positive change, it allows for legal advice to be provided during the epidemic by means of distance communication[13]. It is worth considering and consulting clinic coordinators and students to apply such a solution also in student legal information clinics. It should be borne in mind that law clinics must take care of a high professional level, which is allowed by the rule of using written form. However, the promising forecasts on online law clinics presented by F. Ryan show that, under certain conditions, the provision of legal

11 I. Jarosz, M. Hadel, *Współczesne problemy poradnictwa prawnego na przykładzie działalności Studenckiej Poradni Prawnej UJ – kwestie de lege lata i de lege ferenda*, Internet Legal Review TBSP UJ 2017/8, p. 91.

12 Supreme Audit Office, *Funkcjonowanie systemu nieodpłatnej pomocy prawnej*, ref. no. 4/2018/P/17/090. Own research on a group of 73 potential beneficiaries conducted in 2018–2019.

13 Art. 28a introduced by the amendment of 13 March 2020: In the event of an epidemic emergency, an epidemic, or the introduction of a state of emergency, the provision of free legal aid or the provision of free civic counseling may take place via means of distance communication and outside the premises of the unit.

advice by students online is possible and effective[14]. The Student Legal Information Clinic operating as part of the Faculty of Law and Economics introduced the possibility of obtaining legal advice by e-mail already in the previous academic year, it was positively perceived by the beneficiaries and should be continued. For several decades, student legal information clinics have been operating in a certain legal vacuum[15], universities do not have the power to include law clinics in the statutory free legal aid system, however, within their competences, they should contribute to their development. For this reason, the Library of the Faculty of Law and Economics of the Pedagogical University is constantly expanding the collection of professional literature, which, as well as access to legal information systems, can be used by students providing free legal aid. Among the recommendations regarding the further functioning of university clinics, including the Student Legal Information Clinic of the Pedagogical University, one can also mention an increase in the number of trainings and seminars, and expansion of activities promoting the clinics also outside the Internet,[16] as well as the involvement of students in activities in the field of legal education (aimed at increasing legal awareness by disseminating knowledge on access to free legal aid, civic rights and obligations, possibility of mediation, among others by means of open lectures and workshops).

Summarizing the above considerations, it should be stated that university legal information clinics, regardless of whether the legislator decides to formally incorporate them into the free legal aid system, constitute a significant part of it.

Literature

Bradway J. S., *The nature of a legal aid clinic,* "Southern California Law Review" 1930, Vol. III.

Bradway J. S., *The legal aid clinic: A means of building tough mental fiber,* "Southern California Law Review" 1931, Vol. V.

Du Plessis M. A., *Clinical legal education: Determining the mission and focus of a university law clinic and required outcomes, skills & values,* "De Jure" 2015, Vol. 48, No. 2.

14 F. Ryan, *A virtual law clinic: A realist evaluation of what works for whom, why, how and in what circumstances?* "The Law Teacher" 2020, Vol. 54, No. 2, p. 248.

15 F. Zoll, *O „klinicznej" metodzie nauczania prawa,* "Clinic" 1999, No. 1, p. 40.

16 As shown by the audit of the Supreme Audit Office, the most effective forms of informing about the possibility of using free legal aid were information provided between interested persons (34 %), obtained in a social welfare center (28 %) and in a commune/city office (22 %). Methods involving the use of the Internet proved to be ineffective. Also, a small number of beneficiaries (11 %) indicated that such information came from the press, radio and television. (Information on the results of the inspection, reg. No. 4/2018/P/17/090).

Foundation of *University Legal Clinics, Annual report on the activities of the clinics in the 2018/2019 academic year of 5 February 2020,* Electronic access: http://www.fupp.org.pl/co-nowego/9-polski/aktualnosci/295-roczne-sprawozdanie-z-dzialalnosci-poradni-w-roku-akademickim-2018-2019 (accessed: 10.12.2020).

Jarosz I., Hadel M., *Współczesne problemy poradnictwa prawnego na przykładzie działalności Studenckiej Poradni Prawnej UJ – kwestie de lege lata i de lege ferenda,* "Internet Legal Review TBSP UJ" 2017, no. 8.

Ryan F., *A virtual law clinic: A realist evaluation of what works for whom, why, how and in what circumstances?* "The Law Teacher" 2020, Vol. 54, No. 2.

Supreme Audit Office, *The functioning of the system of free legal aid, ref. no. LOP 430.001.2018, no. 4/2018/P/17/090.* Electronic access: https://www.nik.gov.pl/kontrole/P/17/090/ (accessed: 10.12.2020).

Szewczyk M., *Idea uniwersyteckich poradni prawnych,* "Clinic" 1999, No. 1.

Zoll F., *O „klinicznej" metodzie nauczania prawa,* "Clinic" 1999, No. 1.

Free legal aid – Polish legal solutions

Andrzej Bisztyga[1] and Anna Chodorowska[2]

Normative and jurisprudence grounds for entitling free legal aid in the Constitution of the Republic of Poland

Abstract; The aim of the chapter is to present the constitutional entourage of the institution of free legal aid. On the one hand, free legal aid constitutes an instrument supporting the implementation of the constitutional right to a fair trial (art. 45 of the Constitution RP) and the right to defense, and on the other hand, this instrument itself has the character of a social entitlement. The research reveals the social dimension of the constitutional right to a fair trial. The scope of the study primarily covers the relevant norms of the Constitution RP, including those with the status of supreme principles of the Constitution RP and the selected jurisprudence of the Constitutional Tribunal built around these norms. This includes the constitutional principles of inherent, inalienable human dignity (art. 30 of the Constitution RP), social justice (art. 2 of the Constitution RP) and equality before the law (art. 32 of the Constitution RP). As a supporting element, the research material was also provided by the constitutionally registered obligations of the state and public authorities, having a social nature, such as the obligation to protect the family (art. 18, art. 71 of the Constitution RP) or the obligation to provide aid to people with disabilities in securing their existence, preparing for work and in social communication. Nevertheless, the undertaken research issue reflects on the basis of European law, hence the need to take into account the relevant jurisprudence of the ECtHR in the study. The conducted scientific analysis allows to determine the constitutional foundations and framework of the subjective and objective scope of free legal aid.

Keywords: free legal aid, constitutional right to a fair trial, constitutional social rights

1. Introduction

The aim of this study is to present the standards of free legal aid on the constitutional grounds. Due to the effectiveness of the system of providing this aid, it is

1 University of Zielona Gora. ORCID: 0000-0002-6579-9656.
2 University of Zielona Gora. ORCID: 0000-0002-9660-4049.

justified not only to present this law theoretically, but also to refer to the practical elements of its functioning by referring to the jurisprudence, including the constitutional jurisprudence and the ECtHR.

The following methods were used: legal-dogmatic, legal-comparative, and also descriptive. In the methodological aspect, the purpose of a more comprehensive and descriptive and innovative approach to the subject was the systemic analysis and the analysis of the content, mainly of legal texts. Attention was focused on the norms, standards and constitutional guarantees of free legal aid, also based on the analysis of the case law. The conducted research analysis aims to define the constitutional grounds and the scope of free legal aid.

2. Constitutional guarantees of free legal aid

Undoubtedly, the starting point for the issue of constitutional guarantees of the legal aid system is art. 45 (1) of the Constitution RP. Therefore, free legal aid is an instrument supporting the implementation of the constitutional right to a fair trial, which was emphasized in the constitutional jurisprudence[3]. P. Sarnecki emphasizes that: "the right to a court as an individual's personal right cannot be separated from the right to a court as a guarantee of rights and freedoms, and the attributes of the court as a guaranteed institution cannot be separated from the organizational and functional principles of courts contained in the provisions on their system"[4]. The right to a fair trial is a subjective right of an individual, which is part of the concept of the rule of law. The primary purpose of this law is to provide legal protection and ensure legal security to an individual[5]. Thus, as it is emphasized in the jurisprudence that this right should be effective and should guarantee in practice the proper administration of justice, based on the principle of legal certainty[6]. The Constitutional Tribunal noted that "the right to a fair trial plays an important role in a democratic society and cannot be superficial or theoretical, but

3 Compare: judgments of CT of: 21 July 2009, K 7/09, OTK ZU No. 7/A/2009, item 113, 1 July 2008, SK 40/07, OTK ZU No. 6/A/2008, item 101; 16 June 2008, P 37/07, OTK ZU No. 5/A/2008, item 80, 2 October 2006, SK 34/06, OTK ZU No. 9/A/2006, item 118, 29 August 2006, SK 23/05, OTK ZU No. 8/A/2006, item 94, 16 January 2006, SK 30/05, OTK ZU No. 1/A/2006, item 2.

4 P. Sarnecki, *Art. 45,* [in:] L. Garlicki, M. Zubik (eds.), *Konstytucja Rzeczypospolitej Polskiej. Komentarz,* vol. II, Warszawa 2016, p. 243.

5 M. Augustyniak, [in:] M. Chmaj (ed.), *Wolności i prawa człowieka w Konstytucji Rzeczypospolitej Polskiej,* Warszawa 2016, p. 1087.

6 The judgment of the CT of 12 March 12002, P 9/01, OTK no. 3/1999, item 36; 16 March 1999, SK 19/98, OTK no. 3/1999, item 36. More on this subject: Z. Czeszejko-Sochacki, *Prawo do sądu w świetle Konstytucji Rzeczypospolitej Polskiej (ogólna charakterystyka),* „Państwo i Prawo" 1997, no. 11–12, p. 87, J. Oniszczuk, *Constitution of the Republic of Poland in the jurisprudence of the Constitutional Tribunal at the beginning of the 21st century,* Kraków 2004, p. 723.

effective and practical. (...) Excessive cost barrier may hinder access to the decision of a case by the court (verifying the decision of a non-judicial body by the court), transforming into a disproportionately painful or even prohibitive fee"[7].

In fact, art. 45 of the Constitution RP does not formulate explicitly the requirements for granting legal aid, but states that everyone has the right to a court, especially people who are in a difficult financial situation[8]. The subjective scope of this provision is very wide and covers persons who, due to their financial situation, are not able to bear the costs related to access to court, including the costs of professional legal aid. Undoubtedly, the issue of legal aid is related to the right to a fair trial, and in particular one of its elements in the form of the right of access to a court[9]. As emphasized in the doctrine and jurisprudence, free legal aid is therefore a comprehensive system of support provided to the parties to the proceedings. Otherwise, it could constitute a violation of the right to a fair trial and the principle of equality, in particular, it could constitute a closure of the court procedure that everyone is entitled to, regardless of the existence and content of the substantive legal relationship and the resulting rights[10].

It should be emphasized that guaranteeing access to a court must consider the provisions of the Constitution RP in art. 32 the principle of equality and the prohibition of discrimination on any grounds, including for pecuniary (material) reasons)[11]. According to the constitutional principle of equality, everyone is equal before the law and has the right to equal treatment by public authorities. Moreover, the Constitution RP also prohibits discrimination on any grounds in political, social or economic life. Therefore, the legislator has been obliged to ensure the right to a fair trial for everyone, with due regard for all subjective differences of a given individual. Restrictions in this respect may be justified only by the circumstances indicated in art. 31 (3) of the Constitution RP[12]. Therefore, the legislator has been obliged to ensure the right to a fair trial for everyone, with due regard for all

---

7 Judgment of the CT of 15 April 2014, SK 12/13, OTK ZU no. 4/A/2014, item 41. On the right to a fair trial in the context of the principle of equality and the prohibition of discrimination on financial grounds, see the judgment of the CT of 29 August 2006, SK 23/05, OTK ZU no. 8/A/2006, item 94 and the judgment of the ECtHR of 26 April 2018 in the case of Sępczyński v. Poland, application no. 78352/14.

8 M. Jaworska, *Prawo do sądu*, [in:] M. Jabłoński (ed.), *Realizacja i ochrona konstytucyjnych wolności i praw jednostki* w *polskim porządku prawnym,* Wrocław 2014, p. 148.

9 Ibidem, p. 144. On the scope of the right to a fair trial and its elements see: O. Hołub-Kowalczyk, M. Jabłoński, M. Radajewski, *Identyfikacja treści prawa do sądu – Selected Issues*, Wrocław 2019.

10 P. Mijal, *Nieodpłatna pomoc prawna jako realizacja prawa do sądu*, „Edukacja Prawna" 2012, no. 12, p. 42.

11 https://www.rpo.gov.pl/pl/content/zast%C4%99pca-rpo-stanis%C5%82aw-trociuk-na-temat-nieodp%C5%82atnej-pomocy-prawnej (accessed: 13.11.2023).

12 Ibidem.

subjective differences of a given individual. For this reason, the title right should also apply to those entities which, due to the economic situation, could have limited access to justice[13]. Provision of legal aid in this aspect is related to the principle of equality, both in formal and material terms, relating to the equalization of opportunities for the poorest in accessing the protection of their legal interests[14].

This is undoubtedly related to the principle of a democratic state ruled by law, expressed in art. 2 of the Constitution RP, which is a constitutional guarantee of legal aid, relating to, inter alia, to values such as social justice and equality[15]. This was also emphasized by the CT in its judgment of 8 November 2001 (P 6/01), stating that "under art. 45 of the Constitution, the intention of the legislator is unequivocally clear to include the right to a fair trial to cover the widest possible scope of the case, while the principle of a democratic state ruled by law implies an interpretative directive prohibiting a restrictive interpretation of the right to a fair trial"[16]. At the same time, the constitutional jurisprudence emphasizes that the widest possible access to legal aid is a constitutional value that does not conflict with the principle expressed in art. 17 of the Constitution and the related powers of the professions of public trust. The Constitutional Tribunal is of the opinion that "there are clear social reasons for extending citizens' access to professional legal aid"[17], and "the legislator should open the possibility of providing legal aid to a limited extent by persons who have graduated from higher law studies and obtained the professional title of Master of Laws"[18]. Current is the statement that "outside the sphere of professional activity of lawyers and legal advisers, there is – as indicated – even a number of other areas related to the provision of legal aid. The needs related to the provision of free legal aid to those social groups who cannot afford to pay for a solicitor or attorney must not be lost sight of either. This type of legal aid is provided, for example, by university Law Clinics, foundations or associations specializing in legal aid in the environment of poor, disabled people and requiring support in various spheres of life"[19]. The CT in its judgment of 7 January 1992 (K 8/91) defined the right to a fair trial as "one of the fundamental assumptions of a democratic state ruled by law"[20]. As emphasized in the doctrine, the provision of

---

13 See O. Hołub, *Konstytucyjne gwarancje prawa do nieodpłatnej pomocy prawnej na etapie przedsądowym*, „Forum Prawnicze" 2016, no. 4(36), pp. 70–71, More in: B. Przywora, *Normatywny model przedsądowej nieodpłatnej pomocy prawnej w Polsce*, Warszawa 2019.

14 P. Tuleja, *Zastane pojęcie państwa prawnego*, [in:] S. Wronkowska (ed.), *Zasada demokratycznego państwa prawnego w Konstytucji RP*, Warszawa 2006, pp. 51–72.

15 The judgment of CT of 8 November 2001, P.6/01.

16 The judgment of the CT of 19 April 2006, K 6/06, OTK ZU No. 4/A/2006, item 45.

17 The judgment of the CT of 21 May 2001, K 30/01, OTK ZU No. 3/A/2002, item 32.

18 The judgment of the CT of 26 November 2003, SK 22/02, OTK ZU No. 9/A/2003, item 97.

19 The judgment of the CT of 7 January 1992, K 8/91.

20 O. Hołub-Kozłowska, *Nieodpłatna...*, p. 155.

free legal aid is one of the basic elements guaranteeing the right to a fair trial in a democratic state ruled by law[21]. Free legal aid is inherently related to real access to justice and the related standards of a democratic state ruled by law[22], including the principles of procedural fairness[23]. The most recent constitutional jurisprudence strongly emphasizes the principle of procedural fairness as – resulting from both art. 45 (1) and art. 2 of the Constitution RP, "a value in itself"[24] and a model for the control of the constitutionality of law[25].

It should be noted that this principle was also referred to in the explanatory memorandum to the draft law on free legal aid of 2014, stressing that the property status may not constitute an obstacle to access to justice or to defend the rights and interests of citizens[26].

In one of its judgments, the Constitutional Tribunal stated that "the problem of legal aid for the poor has a constitutional rank and the rank resulting from international standards of human rights protection which are binding for Poland"[27]. Therefore, the basic instrument for the implementation of this obligation of the state authorities, including ensuring the right to a fair trial, is free legal aid[28].

In criminal cases, an individual's right to legal aid has been expressly stated in art. 42 (2) of the Constitution RP, which stipulates that anyone against whom criminal proceedings are conducted has the right to defense at all stages of the proceedings. He may choose a defense lawyer or, on the terms specified in the law, use a public defender. On the other hand, the Constitution RP does not formulate any substantive legal premises on which the emergence of the right to use an ex officio defender depends, referring in this respect to ordinary legislation[29].

---

21 B. Przywora, *Normatywny...*, p. 14.

22 B. Przywora, *Normatywny...*, p. 55. More on this topic: T. Ereciński, *Znaczenie francuskiego Code de procédure z 1806 r. dla rozwoju procesu cywilnego w Polsce*, „Czasopismo Prawno-Historyczne" 2005, vol. LVII, p. 133.

23 See e.g., judgments of the CT of: 1 July 2008, SK 40/07, OTK ZU No. 6/A/2008, item 101; 16 January 2006, SK 30/05, OTK ZU No. 1/A/2006, item 2; 2 October 2006, SK 34/06, OTK ZU No. 9/A/2006, item 118.

24 See e.g., the judgment of the CT of 21 July 2009, K 7/09, OTK ZU No. 7/A/2009, item 113.

25 O. Hołub, *Konstytucyjne...*, p. 71.

26 The judgment of the CT of 29 August 2006, SK 23/05. Similarly, the CT in its judgment of 26 November 2003, SK 22/02.

27 O. Hołub, *Konstytucyjne...*, p. 68.

28 Ombudsman, *Free legal aid*, https://www.rpo.gov.pl/pl/content/zast%C4%99pca-rpo-stanis%C5%82aw-trociuk-na-temat-nieodp%C5%82atnej-pomocy-prawnej (accessed: 13.11.2023).

29 The judgment of the CT of 29 August 2006, SK 23/05, OTK ZU No. 8/A/2006, item 94; see also K. Gonera, *Commentary to the act on court costs in civil cases*, Warsaw 2007, pp. 27 and 566; G. Rząsa, *Konstytucyjne aspekty pomocy prawnej udzielanej osobom ubogim*, „Przegląd Legislacyjny" 2005, No. 3–4, p. 33; see also S. Trociuk, *Pomoc prawna dla osób ubogich jako forma zapewnienia skutecznego dostępu do krajowego*

Selected economic and social freedoms and rights are another constitutional basis for granting free legal aid.

The Constitutional Tribunal, referring to the views of the science of law, notices that legal aid under the Constitution may also be treated as an element of the implementation of the right to social security under art. 67 of the Constitution RP[30]. The implementation of the social right to social security has significant economic consequences[31]. This article provides for the right of a citizen to social security in the event of incapacity to work due to illness, invalidity and after reaching the retirement age, as well as for a citizen who is unemployed not willingly and without any other means of subsistence[32]. It should be noted that social security is "the entirety of benefits that – from public funds – are granted to a citizen in need"[33]. In the historical development of the concept of this law there is an element of the so-called the rights of the poor, which in the light of art. 67 of the Constitution RP, we can refer to free legal aid[34]. The scope and forms of this security are specified by law, there are no obstacles for the legislator to treat legal aid as a form of exercising the constitutional right to social security[35]. The elements of social security include, inter alia, social security, social provision and social aid[36]. This aid is aimed at ensuring a minimum of social security for everyone, based on the

---

i europejskiego wymiaru sprawiedliwości, [in:] *Dostęp obywateli do europejskiego wymiaru sprawiedliwości*, Warszawa 2005. Pursuant to the resolution of the Supreme Court, III CZP 14/00 "in our legal system (unlike in many other countries), both the need to provide a poor person with social aid in the form of exemption from court fees due to the State, and the appointment of an attorney, are not decided by the authorities whose task is to provide this help, but the courts (...); Therefore, since the tasks of courts, as organs separate from the executive authority – the judiciary (Art. 10 (1) of the Constitution RP), include the administration of justice, the obligation imposed on courts to provide social aid to persons applying for legal protection undoubtedly exceeds the scope of these tasks" (Resolution of the Supreme Court of 21 September 2000, OSNC No. 2/2001, item 21).

30 A. Bisztyga, B. Przywora, *Prawa socjalne i ich ochrona w świetle Konstytucji Rzeczypospolitej Polskiej*, [in:] A. Hauser, M. Urbaniak (eds.), *Ochrona praw człowieka. Zagadnienia praktyczne*, Poznań 2019, pp. 21–22.

31 P. Kuczma, *Prawo do zabezpieczenia społecznego*, [in:] M. Jabłoński (ed.), *Realizacja i ochrona...*, p. 598.

32 L. Garlicki, *Komentarz do art. 67* [in:] L. Garlicki (ed.), *Konstytucja Rzeczypospolitej Polskiej. Komentarz*, vol. 5, Warszawa 2007, pp. 3.

33 G. Uścińska, *Świadczenia z zabezpieczenia społecznego w regulacjach międzynarodowych i polskich. Studium porównawcze*, Warszawa 2005, pp. 52.

34 J. Jończyk, *Prawo zabezpieczenia społecznego*, Kraków 2006, p. 30. See also the judgment of the CT of 19 November 1996, K 7/95.

35 https://www.rpo.gov.pl/pl/content/zast%C4%99pca-rpo-stanis%C5%82aw-trociuk-na-temat-nieodp%C5%82atnej-pomocy-prawnej (accessed: 13.11.2023).

36 Ibidem and A. Witkowska, *Przegląd przepisów zawierających odniesienia dotyczące poradnictwa prawnego i obywatelskiego*, Warszawa 2012, pp. 10–11.

constitutional axiology, especially on the principles of social justice and equality[37]. One of the components of this aid under the Act on Social Aid is the so-called specialist counseling, including legal counseling[38]. This confirms the wording contained in art. 4 sec. 1 point 1 of the Act on free legal aid and legal education[39].

Moreover, some indirect constitutional grounds for the guarantee of free legal aid can be found in the regulations concerning the right to property (art. 64 of the Constitution RP), as well as the obligation of public authorities to protect consumers (art. 76 of the Constitution RP)[40], although they do not clearly show the need to extend the guarantees to the poorest. This, however, may indirectly relate to the establishment and operation of the system of free legal aid, including legal counseling[41].

Because of the Constitution, it is also possible to define a group of entities whose situation entitles them to special treatment in the field of access to free legal aid. These include people with disabilities (art. 69 of the Constitution RP), families in a difficult financial and social situation, especially large and incomplete families (art. 71 (1) of the Constitution RP), mothers before and after childbirth (art. 71 (2) of the Constitution RP), children deprived of parental authority (art. 72 (2) of the Constitution RP).

Thus, free legal aid also has a social aspect, such as the obligation to protect the family (art. 18, art. 71) or the obligation to provide aid to disabled people in securing their existence, getting ready for work and in social communication.

The constitutionally guaranteed principle of the good of the family and its legal protection and care, therefore, also includes the material aspect and is related to ensuring its proper functioning through appropriate social and economic policy[42]. Pursuant to art. 71 (1) sentence 2 of the Constitution RP, it is the duty of public authorities to provide special aid to families in a difficult financial and social situation[43]. Undoubtedly, such special aid for such families is free legal aid.

---

37 The catalog of beneficiaries of free legal aid is included in art. 4 of the Act on free legal aid and legal education. It consists of 7 categories of entities that are eligible for legal aid. They are: recipients of social aid benefits during the 12 months preceding applying for free legal aid, the holder of the Large Family Card, a veteran, a war veteran, a person before the age of 26 and after 65, as well as one who found themselves in situations of danger or has suffered losses as a result of a natural disaster, natural disaster or technical failure.

38 O. Hołub, *Konstytucyjne...*, p. 77.

39 Including consumer advisory system – more on this topic J. Węgrzyn, *Prawo konsumenta do informacji w Konstytucji RP i w prawie unijnym*, Wrocław 2013.

40 See commentary on art. 18 and 71 of the Constitution RP – B. Banaszak, *Konstytucja...*, pp. 152, 423.

41 Judgment of the CT of 15 November 2005, P 3/05, OTK ZU no. 10/A/2005, item 115.

42 https://www.rpo.gov.pl/pl/content/zast%C4%99pca-rpo-stanis%C5%82aw-trociuk-na-temat-nieodp%C5%82atnej-pomocy-prawnej (accessed: 13.11.2023).

43 International Covenant on Civil and Political Rights opened for signature in New York on 19 December 1966 (Journal of Laws 1977, No. 38, item 167).

In the justification of the judgment of the CT of 22 November 2004 (SK 64/03), it was stated that "without questioning the importance of professional aid in the course of court proceedings, and consequently – its importance for the exercise of the right to a fair trial, attention should be paid, that the Constitution – apart from criminal proceedings – does not guarantee legal aid. On the other hand, the provisions regulating civil proceedings only to a very narrow extent (...) introduce the so-called coercion of a lawyer, i.e., they make the possibility of performing certain activities conditional on the participation of a professional attorney. In the light of these observations, it is difficult to justify the general thesis on the constitutional right to legal aid of an attorney or legal advisor"[44].

The constitutional jurisprudence recalled that the Constitution itself does not guarantee a universal subjective right to legal aid, including free aid. However, as already indicated, its norms prohibit discrimination in access to court on property grounds. They also require special aid to be provided to the entities mentioned *expressis verbis* in the Constitution. Therefore, failure to take any legislative action or to undertake such action to a degree insufficient from the point of view of these entities' access to a court would consequently have to be considered a violation of the constitutional right of access to a fair trial[45].

3. International guarantees of free legal aid

International regulations also play an important role in determining the minimum standard of legal aid. Pursuant to art. 14 sec. 1 of the International Covenant on Civil and Political Rights, all people are equal before courts and tribunals[46]. The pact also guarantees a person accused of a crime the right to receive information, and if such person does not have a defense lawyer, the existence of the right to have a lawyer designated for him or her whenever the interests of justice so require, without incurring the costs of defense in cases where the accused does not have sufficient funds to cover them[47]. A similar solution regarding criminal

---

44 Judgment of the CT of 22 November 2004, SK 64/03.

45 On this topic: A. Kulikowska, *Prawo do pomocy prawnej w świetle orzecznictwa Europejskiego Trybunału Praw Człowieka*, „Studenckie Zeszyty Naukowe" 2016, Vol. XIX, no. 30.

46 *Handbook of European Law on Access to Justice* https://www.echr.coe.int/Documents/Handbook_access_justice_POL.pdf(accessed: 13.11.2023).

47 See among others: ECtHR judgment of 27 November 2008, no. 36391/02, Salduz v. Turkey, of 13 January 2010, no. 7377/03, Dayanan v. Turkey, of 14 October 2010, no. 1466/07, Brusco v. France, 11 December 2008, no. 4268/04, Panovits v. Cyprus, 26 August 2008, no. 14565/04, VP Diffusion Sarl v. France, 26 February 2002., no. 46800/99, Del Sol v. France, 9 October 1979, no. 6289/73, Airey v. Ireland, no. 26 February 2002, no. 38784/97, Morris v. the United Kingdom.

proceedings is contained in art. 6 (3) lit. c of the ECHR[48]. It provides that each accused of committing a criminal offense, if he/she has insufficient funds to cover the costs of defense, has the right at least to use the free aid of an ex officio-appointed defense lawyer, if it is required by the interest of the justice system. Therefore, it is the obligation of public authorities to ensure access to free legal aid in a situation where an individual, due to his financial situation, cannot effectively assert his rights[49]. This is also reflected in the Strasbourg jurisprudence[50].

The ECHR, as confirmed by case law, applies to the right to free legal aid in both criminal and civil matters[51]. Pursuant to art. 14 of the ECHR, the enjoyment of the rights and freedoms enshrined in the Convention should be ensured without discrimination, inter alia for financial reasons[52]. The ECtHR confirmed, despite the literal reading of art. 6 (1) of the ECHR, the possibility of obtaining legal aid in civil matters. In particular, in a situation where the use of a professional attorney is necessary to guarantee effective access to a court. Consequently, in the judgment of Airey v. Ireland, the ECtHR extended the requirement of legal representation also in civil proceedings[53]. In addition, according to the Committee of Ministers Recommendation No. R (93) 1z on 8 January 1993 on effective access to law and justice people in a situation of extreme poverty, and in the report to this recommendation indicated that the problem of effective access of the poor to the law and the administration of justice is not only a matter of social justice and state policy, but also, and perhaps above all, issues inherent in the guarantees of human rights protection. Moreover, they emphasize that effective and practical access to justice presupposes providing legal aid to persons appearing in all stages of the proceedings and before various judicial authorities[54]. It was also noted that legal aid covers not only partial or total exemption from court costs or free or symbolically paid help of a professional attorney, but also all information, advice, mediation etc. received free of charge, at every stage of the proceedings, as well as quasi course[55].

It should be noted that the Polish constitutional jurisprudence also referred to the recommendation of the Committee of Ministers of 1993. The Constitutional Tribunal in case P 4/0478 on the constitutionality of the provisions of the Civil Code concerning exemption from court costs in land and mortgage register proceedings

---

48 Handbook of European Law on Access to Justice https://www.echr.coe.int/Documents/Handbook_access_justice_POL.pdf (accessed: 13.11.2023).

49 Art. 14 of the ECHR.

50 The judgment of the ECtHR of 9 October 1979, no. 6289/73, Airey v. Ireland.

51 B. Przywora, A. Wróbel, *Poradnictwo...*, p. 2 8.

52 https://www.rpo.gov.pl/pl/content/zast%C4%99pca-rpo-stanis%C5%82aw-trociuk-na-temat-nieodp%C5%82atnej-pomocy-prawnej (accessed: 13.11.2023).

53 B. Przywora, A. Wróbel, *Poradnictwo obywatelskie w świetle badań prawnoporównawczych*, Warszawa 2020, p. 28.

54 *Handbook of European Law on Access to Justice* https://www.echr.coe.int/Documents/Handbook_access_justice_POL.pdf (accessed: 13.11.2023).

55 art. 47 of the CFR.

referred to this recommendation. stressing its importance for the effective and practical access of the poorest to justice[56]

Moreover, the issue of legal aid has been regulated on the basis of EU law[57]. This is expressed in art. 47 of the CFR. This chapter states that everyone has the possibility to obtain legal advice, to be assisted by a lawyer and representative[58]. Legal aid is provided to those who lack sufficient resources to the extent necessary to ensure effective access to justice. In addition, in line with Directive 2003/8/EC, minimum standards for legal aid in cross-border disputes have been established to improve access to justice in cross-border disputes[59]. This directive concerns the application for legal aid in cross-border disputes by persons who do not have sufficient resources, when such aid is necessary to ensure effective access to justice. According to the recital in the preamble to the directive, legal aid should include legal advice before bringing a case to court, resolving a dispute, aid in bringing a case to court and representation in court, as well as partial exemption from or exemption from litigation costs[58].

4. Conclusions

The constitutional standards indicated in this chapter, as well as international guaranteed standards relating to access to the legal aid system, allow for the formulation of certain general standards and assumptions in relation to the presented issues. Undoubtedly, the issue of the legal aid system in the Polish legal order is rooted in the Constitution RP, especially with regard to the principles of a democratic state ruled by law and the right to a fair trial. Its importance also results from international and EU standards for the protection of individual rights. on the basis of these standards, the doctrine emphasizes that this concept includes both pre-trial proceedings and the stages of proceedings before a court as well as enforcement proceedings. At the same time, the constitutional guarantees of this right are based on the principle of equality, both in its material and formal aspects, which requires public authorities to ensure its effectiveness. Moreover, one can does not lose sight of the social aspect of free legal aid. As the Deputy Ombudsman S. Trociuk noted: “the financial criteria for granting legal aid should take into account, on the one hand, the scale of the actual financial burdens related

56 B. Przywora, *Normatywny...*, p. 126 et seq.

57 Ibidem oraz https://www.rpo.gov.pl/pl/content/zast%C4%99pca-rpo-stanis%C5%82aw-trociuk-na-temat-nieodp%C5%82atnej-pomocy-prawnej (accessed: 13.11.2023).

58 https://www.rpo.gov.pl/pl/content/zast%C4%99pca-rpo-stanis%C5%82aw-trociuk-na-temat-nieodp%C5%82atnej-pomocy-prawnej (accessed: 13.11.2023).

59 P. Mijal, *Nieodpłatna...*, p. 43. An example of such categories of cases could be gross violations of the rights and freedoms of an individual.

to the pursuit of justice, on the other hand, they should take into account the fact that this aid constitutes a specific form of exercising the right to social security"[59].

Therefore, it should be emphasized that free legal aid in the constitutional aspect is an instrument supporting the implementation of the right to a fair trial (art. 45 of the Constitution RP) and the right to defense, at the same time taking into account its social nature. Undoubtedly, it is one of the fundamental elements related to the implementation of the right to a fair trial in a democratic state ruled by law. This instrument is inherently related to the principle of equality and the prohibition of discrimination "for any reason", including property or social status.

This right is extremely important due to its constitutional conditions, as well as the society's need for free legal aid, which should be granted not only due to the material status or financial situation of a given entity, but also what is emphasized in the doctrine, taking into account the essence the importance of the case.

It is by no means an unlimited right to receive free legal aid from the state in all circumstances. However, it should be emphasized that it is the duty of public authorities to create such standards and mechanisms that the entitled entity can use them, after meeting certain conditions in a given situation[60].

Literature

Banaszak B., *Konstytucja Rzeczypospolitej Polskiej,* Komentarz, Warszawa 2012.

Bisztyga A., Przywora B., *Prawa socjalne i ich ochrona w świetle Konstytucji Rzeczypospolitej Polskiej,* [in:] A. Hauser, M. Urbaniak (eds.), *Ochrona praw człowieka. Zagadnienia praktyczne,* Poznań 2019.

Czeszejko-Sochacki Z., P*rawo do sądu w świetle Konstytucji Rzeczypospolitej Polskiej (ogólna charakterystyka),* „Państwo i Prawo“ 1997, nr 11–12.

Garlicki L., *Polskie Prawo Konstytucyjne. Zarys wykładu,* Warszawa 2016.

Garlicki L., Zubik M., *Konstytucja Rzeczypospolitej Polskiej. Komentarz,* t. II, Warszawa 2016.

Hołub O., *Konstytucyjne gwarancje prawa do nieodpłatnej pomocy prawnej na etapie przedsądowym,* „Forum Prawnicze“ 2016, nr 4(36).

Hołub – Kowalczyk O., Jabłoński M., Radajewski M., *Identyfikacja treści prawa do sądu – wybrane zagadnienia,* Wrocław 2019.

Jaworska M., *Prawo do sądu,* [in:] *Realizacja i ochrona konstytucyjnych wolności i praw jednostki* w *polskim porządku prawnym,* red. M. Jabłoński, Wrocław 2014.

Mijal P., *Nieodpłatna pomoc prawna jako realizacja prawa do sądu,* „Edukacja Prawna" 2012, nr 12.

Oniszczuk J., *Konstytucja Rzeczypospolitej Polskiej w orzecznictwie Trybunału Konstytucyjnego na początku XXI w.,* Kraków 2004.

Przywora B., *Normatywny model przedsądowej nieodpłatnej pomocy prawnej w Polsce,* Warszawa 2019.

Przywora B., Wróbel A., *Poradnictwo obywatelskie w świetle badań prawnoporównawczych*, Warszawa 2020.

Tuleja P., *Zastane pojęcie państwa prawnego*, [in:] S. Wronkowska (ed.), *Zasada demokratycznego państwa prawnego w Konstytucji RP*, Warszawa 2006.

Uścińska G., *Świadczenia z zabezpieczenia społecznego w regulacjach międzynarodowych i polskich. Studium porównawcze*, Warszawa 2005.

Jacek Sobczak[1]

Legal aid in the jurisprudence of the Supreme Court of the Republic of Poland

Abstract: The aim of the study is to present the issue of legal aid in the jurisprudence of the Polish Supreme Court. The dogmatic method was used in the work. Polish civil and criminal law lacks coherent and systemic regulations concerning the proper implementation of obligations and recommendations resulting from the binding provisions of the Constitution RP (art. 45 (1), art. 77 (2)). In the international perspective, obligations also arise from the International Covenant on Civil and Political Rights, the ECHR, the CFR, as well as other normative acts of the EU. None of the Polish judicial authorities has a legislative initiative or the possibility of introducing amendments to normative acts, which makes it necessary to raise issues regarding legal aid when resolving specific cases. In the few judgments of the Supreme Court of the Republic of Poland concerning this problem, it is pointed out that legal aid should have a wide scope and include free or symbolically paid legal aid and all free assistance in this regard in the form of information, advice, mediation, including in quasi-judicial proceedings. The judgments also concerned the conditions for refusing to provide free legal assistance and the significance of the normative acts regulating the activities of advocates and legal advisers.

Keywords: legal ail, Supreme Court, human rights, equality before the law, right to a fair trial

1. Introduction

The issue of access to legal aid, provided by a professional lawyer, has long been bothering not only the Polish legislator, but is also a subject of keen interest to legislators of public international law (universal), and has also become the subject of regulations in the regional systems of both the Council of Europe and the EU. Issues concerning international regulations, in the sense of the universal and

1 A judge of the Supreme Court of the Republic of Poland currently retired, director of the Institute of Intellectual Property and Medical Rights at the University of Economics and Humanities in Warsaw. ORCID: 0000-0002-2231-8824.

regional system, were competently and thoroughly analyzed by B. Przywora[2]. Recalling the author's findings, it should be emphasized that both the right to defense and its scope constituted one of the main problems of the EU's legislative activity. It should be noted that its actions are clearly aimed at gradual introduction of a unified standard of citizens' access to the legal aid system and a similar, if not identical, scope of the right to defense in the legal space of the entire EU[3].

It should be remembered, however, that the road to modern standards of free legal aid was started by actions undertaken in the system of the Council of Europe. They were set out in Recommendation No. R (93) 1 of the Committee of Ministers of the Council of Europe to member states of the Council of Europe of the Committee on effective access to law and justice for the poorest, adopted on 8 January 1993 at the 484 meeting of the deputy ministers[4]. The recommendation states that Member States should facilitate access to the law for the poorest by promoting, wherever needed, actions which make the legal community more aware of the problems of the poor[5] in accessing justice. The necessity to support non-governmental organizations in activities aimed at quasi-judicial dispute resolution methods was also indicated. The report accompanying the Recommendation points out that the problem of effective access of the poor to law and justice is not only a question of social justice and state policy, but also belongs to the area of human rights and fundamental freedoms. It was pointed out that effective access to justice presupposes providing assistance to people whose cases are heard in all courts and cannot be understood only as a partial or complete exemption from court costs, as well as free or symbolically paid assistance of a professional lawyer. It has been noted that this term should be understood as meaning any information, legal advice or mediation received free of charge, relating to both judicial and quasi-judicial proceedings[6].

---

2 B. Przywora, *Normatywny model przedsądowej nieodpłatnej pomocy prawnej w Polsce,* Warszawa 2019, pp. 85–162.

3 This is pointed out by R. Rynkun-Werner, *Niezależna adwokatura a efektywna pomoc prawna z urzędu,* Warszawa 2016, p. 15 et seq. This monograph is a slightly changed version of the author's doctoral dissertation, the promoter of which was J. Sobczak, and the reviewers of the late prof. B. Banaszak (UZ) and prof. S. Hoc (UO). It was defended at the Faculty of Law and Administration of the University of Warmia and Mazury in Olsztyn on 24 June 2016.

4 http://euromed-justiceii.eu/files/repository/20090123123822_recR(93)1e.pdf (accessed: 12.12.2021). On this issue, see also A. Witkowska, *Przegląd przepisów zawierających odniesienia dotyczące poradnictwa prawnego i obywatelskiego,* „Instytut Prawa i Społeczeństwa", Warszawa 2012, pp. 5–27. Cf. on the practice of European countries Ł. Bojarski, *Dostępność nieodpłatnej pomocy prawnej – raport z monitoringu,* „Helsińska Fundacja Praw Człowieka", Warszawa 2003, passim.

5 On the understanding of "poor people" and in relation to "extreme poverty" in the human rights dimension, see A. Ploszka, *Publicznoprawny status jednostki skrajnie ubogiej,* Warszawa 2019, pp. 43–67 and 84–129.

6 A. Lach, *Europejska pomoc prawna w sprawach karnych,* Toruń 2007, p. 89 et seq.

The issue of free legal aid has become the subject of numerous discussions and studies[7]. They resulted in subsequent recommendations of the Council of Europe, relating to the issues of legal aid in civil, commercial and administrative matters as well as effective access to law and justice for people in extreme poverty. However, numerous directives of the EU were of significant importance, which cannot be analyzed or even listed here, given their detailed nature, and also because they are not cited in the case law of the Supreme Court and common courts of law. It should also be noted that the problem of free legal aid was the subject of inquiries by the Supreme Court also before drawing attention to this issue in the legal system of both the Council of Europe and the EU. However, it usually concerned not so much access to legal aid as matters relating to the costs of unpaid legal aid provided ex officio. In the Polish legal system, both the need to provide a poor person with relief in the form of exemption from the court costs due to the state, and the appointment of a defender or attorney, are not decided by the authorities whose task is to provide this assistance, but by the courts hearing the case with the participation of persons declaring their impoverishment or, which happens much less often, those who only intend to bring such a case.

2. Free legal aid in the jurisprudence of the Supreme Court under the provisions of the Code of Civil Procedure of 1932

Code of Civil Procedure of 19 December 1932 (the Civil Procedure Code of 1932)[8] took up the problem of free legal aid in art. 112 in section II entitled The Law of the Poor. It states that "the granting of the right to the poor may be claimed by a natural or legal person who demonstrates his complete poverty on the basis of a certificate issued by a public authority on his family status, property and income; it is up to the court to consider this certificate as sufficient evidence of the person's complete poverty".

Against the background of art. 112–125 of the Code of Civil Procedure of 1932, the Supreme Court issued a number of judicates, from which it should be noted the

---

7 Here, in particular, it is worth paying attention to the report by E. Cape (ed.), Z. Namorade, R. Smith, T. Spoken, *Effective criminal defence in Europe*, Antwerpia-Oxford-Portland 2010. On this issue, see also the discussion of the conference R. Rynkun-Werner, *Pomoc prawna z urzędu w postępowaniu karnym w Unii Europejskiej*, „Palestra" 2012, no. 1–2, p. 263 et seq.; P. Libertowski, *Pomoc prawna z urzędu w postępowaniu karnym w Unii Europejskiej*, „Palestra" 2012, no. 3–4, p. 240 et seq.; report prepared at the request of the Ministry of Justice of Holland *Legal Aid in Europe: Nine Different Ways to Guarantee Access to Justice?*, Amsterdam 2014, https://www.hiil.org/projects/legal-aid-in-europe-nine-different-ways-to-guarantee-access-to-justice/ (accessed: 12.12.2021).

8 Journal Of Laws 1932, No. 112, item 934.

judgment of 1 February 1961[9], in which it was stated that "depriving a party of the possibility of defending its rights as a ground for nullity of the proceedings does not occur in the event of merely making it difficult for the party to support the claimed claims or allegations before the court". The point was that the Provincial Court, failing to provide the defendant's attorney, established pursuant to art. 116 of the Code of Civil Procedure of 1932, the possibility of communicating with her personally, hindered the defendant's defense. However, he did not deprive her of the ability to defend her rights. Nevertheless, the Supreme Court considered this impediment to be a breach of art. 218 § 1, 232 § 2 and 326 of the Code of Civil Procedure of 1932, because in order to provide a comprehensive explanation of the points of contention, it was necessary to provide the attorney of the defendant to hold talks with her before the trial necessary to defend her rights. In the justification it was emphasized that an advocate appointed for a party exempt from court costs is not obliged to travel at his own expense to a distant town where that party is staying against his will. This was the case in the case at hand, because the defendant was in prison in Grudziądz, serving a prison sentence there, and the lawyer appointed for her was based in Gdańsk. The Regional Court, as stated in the justification, in this situation should have complied with the lawyer's request and ordered that the defendant be transported to Gdańsk, in order to enable the lawyer to contact the party whose rights he was to defend in the trial. The Supreme Court found the refusal to transport, despite the lawyer's demands, inappropriate, as such a defense would be illusory. He also found that such court proceedings violated the guarantee of the discovery of the truth.

In the judgment of 20 September 1935[10] The Supreme Court stated that the Court of Appeal, which upheld the decision of the District Court in Katowice in closed session on 4 December 1934, by which the defendant was refused to grant the right to the poor, without providing any justification, violated the law, as the decision was served on the defendant's attorney, who requested that a statement of reasons be drawn up, receiving notification that the court was not obliged to justify such a decision. In the cassation appeal, which the attorney then brought, he alleged that art. 112 and 114 of the Code of Civil Procedure of 1932, as well as art. 417, 354 § 1, 371 and 351 of the Code of Civil Procedure of 1932, the Supreme Court concluded that, although art. 376 § 2 of the Code of Civil Procedure of 1932, an order issued without a hearing is served on the parties ex officio and the provisions on judgments should apply accordingly to such decisions, but pursuant to art. 379 of the Code of Civil Procedure of 1932, the written justification is required by the decisions against which the complaint is based. He also noted that the provision, which may be pursuant to art. 424 § 2 of the Code of Civil Procedure of 1932, contested by a cassation appeal, requires a justification, since according to art. 379 of the Code of Civil Procedure of 1932, the decision against which the appeal is

9 IV CR 151/60, Lex No. 1633441.
10 III C 520/35, Lex no. 1633621.

served is to be justified, the more justified the decisions challenged by way of cassation. It was added that an order issued without a hearing is to be served on the parties ex officio, but if it has to be justified, it has to be served with a justification. The lack of such justification is a violation of a number of procedural provisions, in particular art. 112 and 114 § 1 of the Code of Civil Procedure from 1932, on the material conditions for obtaining the right of the poor.

In the judicature of 30 January 1963[11] The Supreme Court stated that the obvious groundlessness of the claim, giving rise to the refusal to exempt the party from court costs, occurs only when it is completely obvious for every lawyer without the need to analyze the case in fact and in law that the claim cannot be considered as undoubtedly contradictory with the fundamental and not subject to different interpretations of the law. He added that such a situation did not take place in the case under examination, in which the decision to refuse the exemption from court fees was issued on the basis of the statements of the statement of claim itself, which, without a thorough legal analysis of the facts, does not make it possible to predict that the claim cannot be accepted. Therefore, the appealed decision to refuse exemption from court costs was annulled and the case was remitted for re-examination, indicating as the basis for the ruling of art. 113 § 2 and 394 § 3 of the Civil Procedure Code from 1932.

It is worth noting, however, that in the judgment of May 14, 1954[12] The Supreme Court, examining the case in which the Opole Voivodeship Court rejected the defendant's objection to the default judgment and at the same time dismissed the application for exemption from court costs, stating that this application does not contain charges, facts and evidence, and how such a request is to be rejected, and the defendant's defense is unfounded. In this state of affairs, the exemption from court fees based on the content of art. 113 § 2 of the Code of Civil Procedure of 1932 was justified. The Supreme Court did not share this view and quashed the decision of the Provincial Court dismissing the application for exemption from court fees to the defendant. In the justification, he stated that the content of the objection does not indicate that the defense of the defendant was actually unfounded.

In the judgment of 2 January 1935[13], the Supreme Court stated that in a situation where cassation proceedings in a specific case are inadmissible under the law, the decision of the second instance court refusing the rights of the poor is also inadmissible. Referring to the issue of the jurisdiction of the court in which the application for the granting of the rights of the poor should be submitted, the Supreme Court in its decision of 8 June 1934[14] stated that pursuant to art. 113 § of the Code of Civil Procedure from 1932, an application for the granting of the rights of the poor must be submitted to the court where it is to be brought, or the case is

11 II CZ 3/63, Lex no. 1634102.
12 I C 96/54, Lex no. 1633556.
13 II C 2200/34, Lex no. 1633645.
14 Ref. Act III C 76/34, Lex no. 1633897.

already pending. Later he repeated the previously known position that pursuant to art. 114 § 2 of the Code of Civil Procedure of 1932, a claim is unfounded only if for each lawyer, without the need for a deeper analysis and without checking and assessing the evidence, it is clear that the claim cannot be accepted. On that occasion, it was found that the party which lodged an application for the granting of the rights of the poor, after having lost a dispute at first instance, was not required to provide circumstances and arguments refuting the findings of the judgment under appeal. Of course, it should be remembered that this judgment was issued on the basis of the legal state in which a cassation appeal against the refusal to grant the right of the poor.

It is worth noting that both under the Code of Civil Procedure of 1932 and in the following decades, the provision of ex officio legal aid was a free social obligation of the bar, which did not result from any statutory regulations. Since the entry into force of the Act of 26 May 1982, the Law on the Bar[15] and the Act of July 6, 1982 on Legal Advisers[16], costs of unpaid legal aid, often in amounts completely incompatible with the workload of attorneys appointed ex officio, are borne by the State Treasury, and paid from the budgetary funds of the courts. This regulation was not reflected in the provisions on the system of courts, nor in the provisions regulating proceedings in civil cases, nor in the Act of 13 June 1967 on court costs in civil cases[17]. However, this issue was regulated in the ordinance of the Minister of Justice of 12 December 1997 on fees for lawyers' activities and fees for activities of legal advisers[18]. This ordinance has expired and the ordinances of 22 October 2015 on fees for attorney's services are in force at present[19] and on fees for legal advisers' activities[20]. The concept adopted both in the law on the bar and in the act on legal advisers, and confirmed in subsequent ordinances of the Minister of Justice on fees for activities, is inconsistent with both art. 1 of the no longer applicable Act of 29 November 1990 on social assistance[21], as well as the content of art. 2 of the later Act of 12 March 2004 on social assistance[22]. Pursuant to art. 19 of the Act on Social Assistance, specialist counseling is the poviat's own task (art. 19 point 2). One should share the view contained in the justification of the resolution of the panel of 7 judges of the Supreme Court of 21 September 2000[23], since the tasks of

15 Journal of Laws 1982, No. 16, item 124, as amended, see art. 29 sec. 1; i.e., Journal of Laws 2020, item 1651.
16 Journal of Laws 1982, No. 19, item 145, as amended See art. 22^3, i.e., Journal of Laws 2020, item 75.
17 Journal of Laws 1967, No. 24, item 110 as amended, i.e., Journal of Laws 2020, item 755.
18 Journal of Laws 1997, No. 154, item 1013 as amended.
19 Journal of Laws 2015, item 1800.
20 Journal of Laws 2018, item 265.
21 Journal of Laws 1998, No. 64, item 414.
22 Journal of Laws 2020, item 1876.
23 Ref. no. III CZP 14/00, OSN C 2001, No. 2, item 21, Lex no. 41972.

the courts, as organs separate from the executive and the judiciary, art. 10 (1) of the Constitution RP, it is necessary to administer justice, the obligation imposed on the courts to provide social assistance and to pay this assistance to persons applying for legal protection, undoubtedly exceeds the scope of these activities. It is also noted that the attorneys appointed by the court for the parties, who intend to appeal against the judgment of the second instance court with a cassation appeal, which the party is not entitled to, have a difficult obligation to explain these issues. In practice, in order to avoid complaints brought by such parties before corporate bodies, lawyers and legal advisers submit inadmissible cassation motions, most often distancing themselves from the party's demands in the first words of such a request that it is submitted "at the express request of the party"[24].

3. Case law of the Supreme Court on free legal aid after the amendment of the Code of Civil Procedure in 1964

The new Code of Civil Procedure enacted on 17 November 1964 did not fundamentally change the existing concept of free legal aid. Very rich, but in fact quite homogeneous jurisprudence of the Supreme Court, in this respect is based on the content of art. 117–123 of the Code of Civil Procedure (in criminal cases, these issues are regulated by art. 623–625 of the Code of Criminal Procedure). These judgments, however, generally do not concern the matter contained in the content of the Free Legal Aid Act.

Out of the few judgments concerning the issues of the aforementioned Act, attention should be paid to the judgment of the Supreme Court of 30 May 2019[25], in the justification for which it was indicated that the basis for dismissing an application for the appointment of an ex officio attorney may not be the use by a natural person of free legal aid or free civic counseling, referred to Free Legal Aid Act, the Supreme Court decided that despite the fact that the regulation this was introduced into the Code of Civil Procedure only on 1 January 2019, it cannot raise any doubts that also before this date, the condition for rejecting an application for the appointment of an ex officio attorney could not have been the use of the indicated

---

24 It should be noted that the Supreme Court in the Criminal Law Division in its decision of 21.06.1996 (V KZ 16/96, OSN KW 1996, No. 7–8, item 41) stated that although in the code of conduct there is no equivalent of art. 116 § 2 of the Code of Civil Procedure, the refusal to exempt from the cassation fee may also be justified by the fact that the cassation appeal is inadmissible by operation of law. This position is not shared by the Civil Law Division of the Supreme Court, see resolution of a panel of 7 judges of the Supreme Court of 21.09.2000, III CZP 14/00, OSN C 2001, No. 2, item 21, Lex No. 41972. It should be added here that art. 116 of the Code of Civil Procedure it no longer applies and art. 126 of the Act of 28 July 2005 on court costs in civil cases, i.e., Journal of Laws No. 2020 item 755.

25 Ref. act V CKS 36/18, Lex No. 2690865.

legal aid in the form of free counseling. It is worth noting that, in the Supreme Court's opinion, the refusal to appoint an ex officio legal attorney for a party does not justify the objection of invalidity of the proceedings as a result of depriving the party of the possibility of defending its rights, as such an application is subject to consideration, pursuant to art. 117 § 5 of the Code of Civil Procedure, if, in the opinion of the court, the participation of a professional attorney is necessary. Only in exceptional circumstances, failure to provide professional assistance of the attorney ex officio may be qualified as invalidating the proceedings because of depriving the party of the ability to defend its rights. The Supreme Court noted that this, however, only applies to cases where the party's behavior shows ignorance of the rules of conduct or clumsiness in the actual or legal complexity of the case. Depriving a party of the opportunity to defend its rights consists in the fact that, due to defective procedural acts of the court or of the opposing party, it could not and did not take part in a significant part of the proceedings, and this is about total deprivation of defense. This deprivation occurs only when the party has not been able to defend its rights at all[26].

A similar position was expressed in the justification of the judgment of the Supreme Court of 9 February 2017[27], stating that the refusal to appoint an ex officio

---

26 Such a position was previously presented in the decision of the Supreme Court of 24 April 2018 (V CZ 28/18, Lex No. 2488966), in which it was stated, inter alia, that when assessing the legitimacy of the application for the appointment of an official one should examine not only the actual ability of the party to act on his own in the pending proceedings, but also the degree of complexity of the case. Any automaticity of evaluation is therefore ruled out. Therefore, failure to appoint a professional attorney ex officio – in a situation where the party's behavior shows ignorance of the rules of procedure or awkwardness leading to the fact that, given the factual or legal complexity of the case, it is not able to use the legal possibilities of its proper conduct – may be qualified as an omission of the court causing invalidity proceedings as a result of depriving a party of the ability to defend its rights. Such judgments were also made before the entry into force of the Free Legal Aid Act. See Supreme Court judgments dated 2 March 2005, III CK 533/04, LEX No. 197647: of 25 May 2005, I CK 773/04, LEX No. 180833 and of 8 December 2009, I UK 195/09, OSNP 2011 No. 13–14, item 190 and the decision of the Supreme Court of 15 May 2007, V CSK 37/07, LEX No. 442585. A similar view was expressed in the decision of the Supreme Court of 17 May 2018, IV CSK 120/18, Lex No. 2515757. The justification of this decision indicated that the dominant view in the Supreme Court's jurisprudence is that the refusal to appoint an ex officio legal attorney for a party does not justify the objection of invalidity of the proceedings as a result of depriving the party of the possibility to defend its rights. Such a request would be considered only if, pursuant to art. 117 § 5 of the Code of Civil Procedure the participation of a professional attorney was necessary in the court's assessment. See Supreme Court judgments of 2 March 2005, III CK 533/04, 12 September 2007, I CSK 199/07; of 16 April 2008, V CSK 564/07; 18 April 2008, CSK 636/07, and the decision of the Supreme Court of 15 May 2007, V CSK 37/07 and 29 April 2009, II CSK 643/08.

27 III CSK 1/16, Lex no. 2252190.

attorney may be qualified as invalidating the proceedings, but only in such a situation where the party's behavior shows awkwardness preventing the use of the legal possibilities of conducting an actual or legally complex case. As a rule, therefore, the refusal to appoint an ex officio attorney does not justify the objection of invalidity of the proceedings as a result of depriving the party of the possibility of defending its rights.

In criminal proceedings, the Supreme Court, in its decision of 27 September 2018[28] stated in the justification that in connection with the binding lawyer and legal advisor's compulsion to draw up an application for the reopening of the proceedings, cassation and a complaint against the judgment of the appellate court (art. 526 § 2, art. 545 § 2 and art. 539 f of the Code of Criminal Procedure), the accused, who does not have an elected defense attorney, may request that he be appointed an ex officio defender, if there are premises for his establishment under art. 78 § 1 or compulsory defense takes place (art. 79 § 1 and 2 of the Code of Criminal Procedure). However, such a situation did not occur in the case at hand. Since there was no legal basis for submitting this content of the application, it was unnecessary to issue an order refusing to consider the application for the appointment of a defense attorney, as its submission should only result in an action of the entity specified in art. 93 § 2 of the CCP of an administrative nature.

A similar view was presented in the justification of the Supreme Court's decision of 19 March 2019[29]. It indicated that applying for the appointment of an ex officio defender does not require legal knowledge and may be limited to a very simple request. Therefore, the convicted person, while taking care to exercise his procedural rights, could submit an appropriate application on time. It cannot be argued that the convicted person was wrong as to the fact that he can still use the assistance of a defense lawyer acting in the appeal proceedings. The convict's awareness that the advocate is no longer obliged to take procedural steps on his behalf is evidenced by the fact that he lodged a personally prepared cassation appeal to the appeal court[30].

---

28 VII KZ 12/18, Lex no. 2572998.

29 IV KZ 5/19, Lex no. 2636194.

30 It is worth noting that in the justification of the Supreme Court dated 11 October 2017 (III KZ 48/17, Lex No. 2390687), it was found that the conviction on the part of the existence of grounds for the appeal cannot justify eject it further requests for appointment another public defender, until her expectations are effectively met by lodging a cassation appeal. This is not how the right to the assistance of an ex officio defender should be understood. The role of this defense counsel is to determine whether or not there are grounds for lodging a cassation appeal. Due to the fact that a cassation appeal is a highly formalized extraordinary means of appeal, only professional entities are entitled to prepare and sign it on behalf of a party who is not able – as a non-professional – to independently assess the existence of the conditions for its submission.

4. Conclusions

The issue of free legal aid was the subject of numerous judicatures of the Supreme Court, both in civil and criminal proceedings. It should be admitted, however, that after the entry into force of the Free Legal Aid Act, few judgments affect the matter regulated in this act and raise the problem of interpreting its provisions. This does not mean, however, that the text of the aforementioned act is not in doubt. The fact that the Supreme Court is extremely cautious about the content of this law is because the parties do not invoke its text in support of their conclusions. Indirectly, this may prove that the act is not overly popularized, and thus known to the people who were to be its beneficiaries. Undoubtedly, this state of affairs will change over time. An in-depth analysis of the content of the act allows one to fear that its authors will, on the one hand, make it available to people who are not able to bear the costs of paid legal aid, on the other, however, it seems that they wanted to provide legal services to graduates of legal studies with the title of Master's degree and at least three years of experience in performing activities requiring legal knowledge, which were not able to get into any of the applications. It can be assumed that the situation will gradually change over time. It seems that much remains to be done in the area of free legal aid. Perhaps it would be advisable to provide legal protection to persons forcibly placed in sobering-up stations, which, according to the judgments of the ECtHR, often go there in Poland without justification and in breach of applicable regulations[31]. Undoubtedly, there is a pressing need to finally resolve the issues of amicus curiae clearly and unambiguously in the Polish legal system. This role was sometimes managed by the Helsinki Foundation for Human Rights or the Human Rights Defender. Recently, such a possibility has been granted to the President of the Office of Competition and Consumer Protection, when he deems it to be in the public interest[32].

Literature

Bojarski Ł., *Dostępność nieodpłatnej pomocy prawnej – raport z monitoringu*, „Helsińska Fundacja Praw Człowieka", Warszawa 2003.

Lach A., *Europejska pomoc prawna w sprawach karnych*, Toruń 2007.

---

31 J. Sobczak, *Uzasadniony zakres interwencji państwa w sferę wolności obywateli*, [in:] T. Gardocka, J. Sobczak (eds.), „Izby wytrzeźwień a prawa człowieka", Toruń 2013, pp. 21–35; W. Sobczak, *Europejski Trybunał Praw Człowieka wobec zatrzymań w izbach wytrzeźwień*, [in:] T. Gardocka, J. Sobczak (eds.), „Izby wytrzeźwień a prawa człowieka", Toruń 2013, pp. 74–91.

32 Pursuant to art. 31 d of the Act of 16 February 2007 on competition and consumer protection (Journal of Laws of 2021, item 275). The legislator, however, did not define this competence as an action of *amicus curiae*.

Libertowski P., *Pomoc prawna z urzędu w postępowaniu karnym w Unii Europejskiej*, „Palestra" 2012, no. 3–4.

Ploszka A., *Publicznoprawny status jednostki skrajnie ubogiej*, Warszawa 2019.

Przywora B., *Normatywny model przedsądowej nieodpłatnej pomocy prawnej w Polsce*, Warszawa 2019.

Report Cape E. (red.), Namorade Z., Smith R., Spoken T., *Effective Criminal Defence in Europe*, Antwerpia-Oxford-Portland 2010.

Report prepared at the request of the Ministry of Justice of Holland *Legal Aid in Europe: Nine Different Ways to Guarantee Access to Justice?*, Amsterdam 2014, https://www.hiil.org/projects/legal-aid-in-europe-nine-different-ways-to-guarantee-access-to-justice/ (accessed: 13.11.2023).

Rynkun-Werner R., *Pomoc prawna z urzędu w postępowaniu karnym w Unii Europejskiej*, „Palestra" 2012, no. 1–2.

Rynkun-Werner R., *Niezależna adwokatura a efektywna pomoc prawna z urzędu*, Warszawa 2016.

Sobczak J., *Uzasadniony zakres interwencji państwa w sferę wolności obywateli*, [w:] T. Gardocka, J. Sobczak (eds.), *Izby wytrzeźwień a prawa człowieka*, Toruń 2013.

Sobczak W., *Europejski Trybunał Praw Człowieka wobec zatrzymań w izbach wytrzeźwień*, [in:] T. Gardocka, J. Sobczak (eds.), *Izby wytrzeźwień a prawa człowieka*, Toruń 2013.

Witkowska A., *Przegląd przepisów zawierających odniesienia dotyczące poradnictwa prawnego i obywatelskiego*, „Instytut Prawa i Społeczeństwa", Warszawa 2012.

Jacek Zaleśny[1]

The right to fair court proceedings and free legal aid

Abstract: The aim of the considerations is to examine the relationship between the constitutional right to fair court proceedings and free legal aid. They put forward a thesis that from the point of view of the implementation of constitutional values, it is not without significance what the legal and factual position of the parties to court proceedings is shaped. The work assumes that the constitutional right to fair court proceedings (art. 45 of the Constitution RP) loses its significance when a participant in legal relations, due to his financial situation, is deprived of the real ability to present his legal and factual reasons to the court at the right moment and to the appropriate extent and as a result his subjective rights are lost. The research question posed is: in the light of the applicable court procedures, is a party (applicant, participant in the proceedings in non-litigious proceedings, respectively) unable to bear the costs of paid legal aid guaranteed free legal aid? In the legal state that is the Republic of Poland, pursuant to art. 2 of the Constitution RP, parties to court proceedings should be able to present their position in a comprehensive manner so that the court deciding the case will establish the substantive truth in the proceedings and issue a fair and just judgment. The study presents the thesis that if, due to material deficiencies, a party (the applicant, participant, respectively) of court proceedings is not able to pay for the help of a professional attorney from their own resources, then – in order to exercise the right to court – it is the duty of public authorities the right to free legal aid.

Keywords: fair court proceedings, subjective rights, free legal assistance

1. Introduction

The aim of the study is to characterize the relationship between the right to fair court proceedings and free legal aid. It states and proves the thesis that free legal aid provided to a party to the proceedings (respectively in non-litigious proceedings to the applicant, participant in the proceedings) who needs it, is necessary

1 University of Warsaw. ORCID: 0000-0002-8231-4454.

for the administration of justice, and thus for building stable social relations. The thesis formulated in this way is proved primarily with the use of a dogmatic method, used together with systemic and functional.

The right to a fair trial is a public subjective right of participants in legal relations. As Cicero and St. Augustine: give everyone their due – this is the highest form of justice. It is this form of justice and, crucially, the only form that is served by the administration of justice by the court. There is no need to administer justice that does not give everyone what is due. It is a contradiction of the administration of justice that should not be pursued in a state ruled by law.

There are a number of conditions that must be met for fair court proceedings to exist. They include both the acts of lawmaking and the acts of applying the law. As far as the acts of law-making are concerned, these are: a properly formed court system, the procedure of court proceedings and the provisions of substantive law applied by the court. Even the most perfectly formed legal regulations themselves are worth little when they are improperly applied, when their application is directed only at resolving the case, and not at bringing justice. The practice of judicial proceedings in modern states shows that this is a fundamental problem. He corresponds to a sense of social resentment and disappointment that by an imperative, unchallenged and unshakeable act, the court on behalf of the state approved the act of injustice, and orders to treat it as if it were an act of justice. Administration of justice, which results in the feeling of large social groups that injustice has been approved, is itself a contradiction and should not take place in a state ruled by law.

2. The right to a court and the costs of court proceedings

A formal condition for a fair trial is to ensure that the right to a fair trial is exercised[2]. In Poland, remuneration of the judiciary was adopted as the principle. The exception is the exemption from court costs and the appointment of a free (for the party, in the non-litigious proceedings of the applicant, participant in the proceedings, respectively) professional attorney/public defense lawyer. In the light of the jurisprudence of the ECtHR (mainly pursuant to art. 6 of the ECHR), free court proceedings do not have to apply to all court proceedings. It is to be used in criminal proceedings and the Polish legislator meets this condition. However, in the light of art. 6 of the ECHR, free court proceedings are not a standard in all administrative and civil court proceedings. At the same time, however, in a specific category of cases (e.g., when the legislator provides for compulsory attorneys-at-law) or when it is justified by the complex nature of the case, the effectiveness of access to fair trial requires the state to guarantee access to free legal aid. In Poland,

2 M. Lewandowski, *Problematyka bezpłatnej pomocy prawnej w RP na tle prawa do sądu*, „Monitor Prawniczy“ 2009, no. 21.

this standard is not only met, but also a further-reaching standard is set. Access to free legal aid also applies to proceedings where it is not necessary under the ECHR.

In Poland, the motive of remuneration of the judiciary, which is important for access to fair trial, has different meanings in various court proceedings. In administrative court proceedings, important from the point of view of building power relations in the state based on the principle of legalism (art. 7 of the Constitution RP), the amount of the permanent fee (e.g., in the scope of complaints regarding concessions, permits or business permits), as well as the relative fee (e.g. depending on the amount of money owed under the contested act) may be a real obstacle to bringing an action before the court. It is similar in civil proceedings. In civil proceedings, the party requesting the court to take specific actions, such as the plaintiff in the trial, the applicant in non-contentious proceedings, or the party lodging an appeal against a court decision, are obliged to pay a court fee. Due to the financial situation, a party to the proceedings may be fully or partially exempted from court costs, and a professional attorney may be appointed for them. At the same time, however, due to the access to fair trial, in some categories of court cases, the legislator exempts persons asserting their rights from paying the court fee. Such a situation occurs, for example, in the area of asserting one's rights under the employment relationship, service relationship, aid or social welfare.

A fair hearing of a case by a court and a fair judgment require taking into account the facts of the parties to the proceedings. In this regard, it is important to distinguish between the participation of a professional entity (professional legal representative) and the participation of non-professional entities in the proceedings. The court has the right to expect and require from professional entities that they know the applicable provisions of law and are Any exceptions in this respect, indicating the unprofessional action of professional legal representatives, should result in the issue being signaled to the body of the relevant professional self-government. On the other hand, a different approach should apply to non-professionals participating in court proceedings. Considering their lack of professionalism, combined with the supreme value of court proceedings (respectively: judicial and administrative) in the form of determining the substantive truth in the proceedings and taking a fair decision, requires the court to take into account their actual ability to express their position in the proceedings in terms of legal issues as well as determining the actual state of the proceedings. For this reason, the legislator provides for free legal aid for the poor.

3. Constitutional framework for free legal aid

Free legal aid[3], provided to participants of court proceedings is based both in the provisions of national law, as well as in international agreements binding Poland and the law of the EU. As B. Przywora insightfully observes, the obligation to

3 On the various sociological observations regarding free legal aid, see A. S. Bartnik, K. J. Kowalska, *Nieodpłatna pomoc prawna,* Warszawa 2019; M. Stefaniuk, *Społeczna*

establish it is anchored directly in the provisions of the Constitution RP[4]. In its preamble, it is solemnly and solemnly assured that the motive for establishing the Constitution RP is, inter alia, guaranteeing civic rights forever, and reliability in the operation of public institutions. There can be no doubt that the obligation to ensure civil rights applies to all spheres of activity of public authorities, and therefore also to the courts; also, the courts are not exempt from activities for the implementation of civil rights, regardless of the social and financial status of citizens, the ability to independently meet their procedural needs. Pursuant to the provision included in the preamble to the Constitution RP in force, not only the rich have the right to seek justice in courts, but also indigent citizens. Administration of justice is therefore to be independent of the social status of a party to the proceedings and during the court proceedings it is to eliminate the negative consequences related to it. In other words, in the light of the binding preamble to the Constitution RP, court proceedings are to ensure the actual equality of the parties/participants in the proceedings in pursuing their rights before the court. The theme of equality is of particular importance in administrative court proceedings, in which there is a confrontation between a public authority and a private law entity, i.e., entities that are essentially unequal. By providing the necessary legal aid, this inequality should be reduced in specific court proceedings; limited, because in the actual state – regardless of the wording of the regulations – it is not subject to elimination. Behind the disputed public authority, there is the administrative apparatus of the state, with its resources (financed from public funds), which can be fully used in this dispute. A body of private law does not have similar factual possibilities. As a rule, unlike a public authority, j bears all costs related to the proceedings through private (and therefore significantly limited) funds. This relevant factual circumstance should be taken into account by the legislator and be reflected in the wording of the legal regulations adopted by him. In my opinion, this circumstance should determine the basis of the court proceedings on the investigation by the court of the substantive truth[5] in the case under examination and the active participation of the court in this process. The same circumstance should limit the adversarial nature of the proceedings by minimizing the risk that the actual inequality of the parties to the proceedings will have an impact on presenting their arguments to the court, and then on issuing an unfair decision by the court. In this regard, it is necessary to apply legal aid and to investigate the substantive truth in the proceedings by the court.

---

potrzeba nieodpłatnej pomocy prawnej – beneficjenci regulacji ustawowej, „Studia Iuridica Lublinensia“ 2016, vol. XXV, No 3.

4 B. Przywora, *Normatywny model przedsądowej nieodpłatnej pomocy prawnej w Polsce,* Warszawa 2019, p. 14 et seq.

5 Regarding the criminal trial, see A. Murzynowski, *Istota i zasady procesu karnego,* Warszawa 1994, p. 27.

Directly in the preamble to the Constitution RP, it was solemnly proclaimed not only that the motive for the establishment of the Constitution is to guarantee civic rights forever, but also that in the Republic of Poland, reliability is a characteristic of the operation of public institutions. There is no doubt that it should also apply to courts as organs of public authority. Pursuant to the preamble to the Constitution RP, the courts are also obliged to diligently perform the tasks entrusted to them. Reliable examination of the entrusted case requires a thorough knowledge of the entirety of its legal and factual status, and only after this condition is met, the authority acting reliably is able to decide. It is not without significance whether the party (respectively: the applicant, participant in the proceedings) to the proceedings was able to express their arguments relevant to the case. If this circumstance is not met due to its properties, a reliable explanation and resolution of the case requires the use of free legal aid on the part of the proceedings.

The contours of the axiology of the Republic of Poland expressed in the preamble to the Constitution RP have been specified and made more specific in its detailed provisions. In the context of the relationship between the right to a fair trial and free legal aid, two regulations are particularly important: art. 2, according to which the Republic of Poland is a state ruled by law and art. 45[6], everyone has the right to a fair hearing by a court. A fair hearing of a case by a court requires that everyone be given what is their due, and for this to happen, it may be necessary to provide a party to the proceedings with free legal aid.

The fair trial standard applies to all cases heard by courts. It is a condition for the effective and actual implementation of the right to a fair trial[7]. Applies to both contentious and non-contentious procedures. It should be emphasized that it applies not only to criminal proceedings, but also to civil, court-administrative, enforcement and security proceedings.

5. Reliable examination of the case and the constitutional principle of equality

Consideration of a fair hearing of a case requires reference to the principle according to which all addressees of legal norms characterized by a given significant feature are to be treated equally, i.e., according to the same measure, without discriminating or favoring differentiation[8]. In the context of court proceedings, the status of a party to the proceedings is the relevant feature to which the equality attribute relates. A party to the proceedings is to be treated impartially by the

6 On the relationship between art. 45 and art. 2 of the Constitution RP, see more in P. Grzegorczyk, K. Weitz, *Komentarz do art. 45,* [in:] Safjan, L. Bosek (ed.), *Konstytucja RP. Tom 1. Komentarz art. 1–86,* Warszawa 2016, pp. 1091–1092.

7 O. Hałub-Kowalczyk, *Sformalizowany model dostępu do nieodpłatnej pomocy prawnej na etapie przedsądowym w Polsce,* Wrocław 2019, p. 39.

8 See e.g., the judgment of the CT of 7 June 2004, P 4/03, OTK ZU no. 6/A/2004, item 55.

court, without any preference or discrimination in relation to the treatment of the other party to the proceedings. At the same time, the principle of equality understood in this way must be placed in the context of the primary function of the court, which is the administration of justice (or taking another act of applying the law). Thus, in court proceedings, equality is not a value, but serves as an auxiliary to the purpose of the proceedings and is considered through its prism. The legislator cannot remain indifferent to the actual inequality of formally equal parties to court proceedings, to the differentiated capacity to articulate their arguments in the proceedings. For this reason, formal equality of the parties to court proceedings coexists with the obligation to maintain substantive equality, i.e., to maintain a similar capacity to express one's legal reasons and arguments relating to the facts. Disruptions in this respect, caused by the properties of a party to the proceedings, are eliminated through free legal aid. In fair court proceedings, it is directed not so much at satisfying the subjective interest of a specific party to the proceedings, but at realizing the objective interest in the form of the public interest. The imposition of fair judgments or the fair exercise of other powers of the court requires a comprehensive outline of the circumstances relevant to a given court proceeding, regardless of the specific predispositions of its parties/participants. If for this purpose it is required to apply compensation mechanisms, they must be used in view of the telos of court proceedings. A similar justification should be presented for the court to establish the substantive truth in the proceedings. If it requires active participation of the court in its investigation, in the state of law in which the courts are called upon to administer justice, and not to determine who was more efficient in the proceedings, who in a more proficient use of legal remedies, the court is obliged to perform the necessary in this area activities.

The constitutionally guaranteed right to a fair trial is universal. Pursuant to art. 45 of the Constitution RP is entitled to "everyone" who falls under the jurisdiction of the Republic of Poland. The quantifier "everyone" clearly and unequivocally defines the subjective side of this right; in particular, the legislator does not allow the situation that the social status of a participant in legal relations, its special properties, may deprive him of the right to a court, either based on acts of lawmaking or in the process of its application[9]. In other words, also poor participants of legal relations have the constitutional right to claim their case in court proceedings. If it would be difficult due to their poor financial situation, this natural obstacle should be removed through free legal aid in the scope of exemption from court costs and appointment of a professional attorney/defender ex officio. As it is noted in the legal doctrine, the provision of free legal aid is not universal. It may only cover those participants in legal relationships for whom payment of the costs of the proceedings is objectively impossible. Thus, it is the

9 A. Kubiak, *Konstytucyjna zasada prawa do sądu w świetle orzecznictwa Trybunału Konstytucyjnego*, Łódź 2006, p. 145; R. Rynkun-Werner, *Niezależna adwokatura a efektywna pomoc prawna z urzędu*, Warszawa 2016, p. 116.

party/participant in the proceedings that is obliged to prove that he or she does not have the means to finance participation in court proceedings[10]. The party to the proceedings fulfills this obligation in the application for legal aid or in documents submitted by the party at the request of the court. In particular, an independent condition for granting free legal aid is not the fact that a party to the proceedings has the status of an unemployed person, a disability pensioner or a pensioner. Each time, the property situation of a party to the proceedings is determined in terms of its current and actual property statu[11]. In this regard, the burden of proof is legitimately on the party seeking the grant of the right, and not on the authority which decides to grant legal aid.

The right to a court is additional, constitutional, in criminal proceedings. Pursuant to art. 42 (2) of the Constitution RP, not only has anyone against whom criminal proceedings are conducted has the right to defense at all stages of the proceedings, but at the same time, expressis verbis in this provision stipulates that he may use an ex officio defender under the terms of the Act. In other words, in criminal proceedings, the conditionally implemented right of free legal aid has direct constitutional anchorage.

6. Differentiation of the status of free legal aid

The provision of free legal aid is subject to differentiation due to the type of court proceedings. It is related to the different nature of the rights of the party (respectively: the applicant, the participant in the proceedings), which are pursued, respectively – may be infringed in each court proceeding. In this research perspective, attention should be paid to court-administrative and criminal proceedings. The essence of the first one is that the subject of private law is in a legal dispute with a public authority, which is backed by the administrative apparatus of the state and all related material and human resources. Another public authority, such as the public prosecutor's office, may join the dispute, and the subject that also resolves the conflict is a public authority in the form of a court. Consideration of fair proceedings against a public authority body and subjective conviction of participants in legal relations that in a dispute against a public authority body the position of a private law entity is equal to the legal position of a public law entity, rationalizes the use of legal aid, including free legal aid.

For other reasons, the use of legal aid is justified in fairly conducted criminal proceedings. As a rule (ignoring the motive for bringing a private indictment) in it, a public authority accuses the citizen of committing a crime, and another public authority adjudicates on this accusation. The possibility of claiming one's rights requires the accused to actively participate in criminal proceedings, for which it

---

10 B. Przywora, *Normatywny...*, p. 52.
11 R. Rynkun-Werner, *Niezależna...*, p. 120.

may be necessary to use legal aid, including free of charge. Otherwise, his freedom and property rights are at risk.

The issue of legal aid is subject to nuance in civil proceedings. When the parties to the proceedings are entities like each other in terms of material resources, not only formal but also material equality of the parties to the proceedings is subject to behavior, and then the issue of legal aid loses its importance. The issue becomes more complicated when the parties to the proceedings are entities that are significantly unequal to each other when the plaintiff is an entity with assets that are a multiple of the defendant's property, or when an organized entity with public funds is suing a natural person. In this type of proceedings, despite the statutory equality of the parties to the proceedings, the defendant does not have equal access to the court and without the help of a professional attorney, his interests may be infringed. Hence the importance in civil proceedings of providing free legal aid in the form of the possibility of appointing an attorney ex officio.

The free legal aid granted to a party to the proceedings (respectively in the non-litigious proceedings of the applicant, a participant in the proceedings), although it serves the exercise of the right to a fair court proceeding, paradoxically – at the same time may result in limiting the right to a court to the extent that its component is the right to obtain a judgment without unnecessary delay. It can also be harmful from the point of view of shaping social relations. This happens when it provokes the irrational use of the right to a fair trial in the form of court fringe or other harassment in order to harass citizens or gain financial benefits. Pleadings concerning manifestly unfounded claims may violate the subjective interests of participants in legal relations, i.e., be incompatible with the rights of the persons to whom they relate. In a situation where they are brought to court in large numbers, they negatively affect the efficiency of the courts and cause lengthy court proceedings, which not only affect the particular rights of the parties to these proceedings, but also infringe the public interest in the form of effective and trusted activity. the courts as the administration of justice. For this reason, the right to free legal aid should apply to the protection of the legitimate interests of a party to the proceedings, i.e., those interests which in a state ruled by law deserve legal protection. Litigation, the use of the right to a fair trial to harass citizens or gain financial benefits, do not have this feature and as such are not protected by law.

The right to a fair trial is not only a constitutionally provided right but is also anchored in international and EU law that is binding on the Republic of Poland. Although the meanings of the "right to a fair trial" they adopt are autonomous in relation to the constitutional understanding of the "right to a fair trial" and there are differences between them (e.g. as to the subjective side of the right to a fair trial and e.g. in the jurisprudence of the ECtHR, Polish maritime chambers are considered courts, while according to the provisions of the Constitution RP, sea chambers do not have this feature), similarly to the Constitution RP – both international law and EU law pay attention to the effectiveness of the implementation of this right. For a party to the proceedings, regardless of the details of the structure of the court proceedings, the right to a fair trial is to ensure effective pursuit of their arguments, i.e., the possibility of expressing all their legal arguments relevant to the case and as to the facts of the case, at the right time and at the right time. appropriate scope, with such consequences that the court will respond to them with full diligence. If for this purpose it is necessary to provide free legal aid, then, for the sake of fair court proceedings, a party to the proceedings should have access to it.

A fair court proceeding requires consideration of the motive of compulsory attorney-at-law. The constitutionality of its application was confirmed by the Constitutional Tribunal, inter alia, in the judgment of 16 October 2002.[12] Its purpose is to ensure professional assertion of the rights of the parties to court proceedings, in the first instance to make the court reject the pleading for formal reasons, but to make it run and then submit it to substantive consideration. Secondly, in a methodologically correct manner, the arguments of the parties to the proceedings will be presented in the proceedings and the court will take a decision without undue delay. In this way, the coercion of an attorney-at-law, serving to pursue the particular interest of the parties to the proceedings, contributes to the formation of the public interest in the form of a fair settlement of the case under examination. The constitutionality of an attorney-at-law coercion does not exclude the choice of a different solution in the form of seeking protection of one's rights by a party to court proceedings on their own. Nevertheless, when it could be subject to the risk of losing the pursuit of rights due to the properties of a party to the proceedings, there are no constitutional obstacles for the application of the advocate-legal coercion. On the constitutional level, there are no contraindications for obligatory professional legal aid to apply not only (as in the applicable legal system) regarding the lodging of extraordinary means of appeal, but also regarding lodging pleadings to the court, court proceedings and enforcement proceedings.

7. Conclusions

The thesis was proved at the hearing that there is a connection between conducted court proceedings and free legal aid. Consideration of a fair, fair, examination of a case (not only a dispute, but also any other case considered by the court) requires attention to be paid to whether the party to the proceedings (the applicant or the participant of the meeting, respectively) meets the conditions for a comprehensive legal and factual expression of their arguments for this purpose. on this basis, having at its disposal all the material relevant for the examination of the case, the court could make a fair decision.

An answer was given to the research question, which was: in the light of the applicable court procedures, a party (in non-contentious proceedings, the applicant, a participant in the proceedings, respectively), who is unable to bear the costs of paid legal aid, is guaranteed free legal aid? If a party to the proceedings, due to their financial conditions, is not able to bear the costs related to the proceedings on

12 Decision of the CT of 16 October 2002, SK 43/01, OTK ZU no. 5/A/2002, item 77.

their own, the purpose of the proceedings in the form of its fair conduct requires the state to grant free legal aid. In the light of the applicable provisions, its scope and intensity are adequate to the specifics of a given procedure, i.e., enable the achievement of its objectives. This means that the scope of free legal aid may be different in various court proceedings, while its standard must be the same, i.e., to the same extent, it should enable the implementation of fair court proceedings.

Literature

Bartnik A. S., Kowalska K. J., *Nieodpłatna pomoc prawna,* Warszawa 2019.

Grzegorczyk P., Weitz K., *Komentarz do art. 45,* [w:] *Konstytucja RP. Tom 1. Komentarz art. 1–86,* red. Safjan, L. Bosek, Warszawa 2016.

Hałub-Kowalczyk O., *Sformalizowany model dostępu do nieodpłatnej pomocy prawnej na etapie przedsądowym w Polsce,* Wrocław 2019.

Kubiak A., *Konstytucyjna zasada prawa do sądu w świetle orzecznictwa Trybunału Konstytucyjnego,* Łódź 2006.

Murzynowski A., *Istota i zasady procesu karnego,* Warszawa 1994.

Przywora B., *Normatywny model przedsądowej nieodpłatnej pomocy prawnej w Polsce,* Warszawa 2019.

Rynkun-Werner R., *Niezależna adwokatura a efektywna pomoc prawna z urzędu,* Warszawa 2016.

Stefaniuk M., Społeczna potrzeba nieodpłatnej pomocy prawnej – beneficjenci regulacji ustawowej, „Studia Iuridica Lublinensia“ 2016, vol. XXV, No 3.

Irena Lipowicz[1] and Radosław Mędrzycki[2]

Role of the Ombudsman in the normalization of free legal aid

Abstract: The Commissioner for Human Rights is a body that actively participates in supporting and promoting free legal aid. It manifested itself in the sphere of participation in the process of creating legal solutions in this area, as well as in monitoring the existing legal solutions. The indicated chapter shows the development of the system of free legal aid from the perspective of the former Ombudsman, who actively participated in activities aimed at improving this institution.

Keywords: The Commissioner for Human Rights, free legal aid, legislation

1. Introduction

All Ombudsmen, since the establishment of this office, were aware of the need to create a system of free legal aid in Poland. Poland's lagging in this area and in terms of mediation in relation to other countries became more and more visible with time, especially after 2000. Numerous initiatives of the Ombudsman's office could alleviate the situation on an ongoing basis but could not heal it. Also, characteristic were the attempts by the Ombudsman to take on the burden of legal education – to raise the general legal culture, undertaken in particular by Adam Zieliński and Andrzej Zoll[3]. The "Codziennik prawny" by Janusz Kochanowski was also supposed to serve this purpose, but the number of its users was gradually decreasing, and in the times of popularization of search engines, a separate system of fairly general information about the law had no better chance. On the other hand, there was a growing demand for profiled, but free of charge, information and legal aid. Persistent efforts to create a universal system of legal aid for people in need were successfully completed by the act – in the summer of 2015. It should

---

1 Cardinal Stefan Wyszyński University in Warsaw. ORCID: 0000-0001-6794-6683.
2 Cardinal Stefan Wyszyński University in Warsaw. ORCID: 0000-0002-9407-4881.
3 A. Zieliński, *Wielkość prawa budujemy wszyscy*, Warszawa 2000, pp. 13–18. A. Zoll, *Państwo prawa jeszcze w budowie*, Warszawa 2013 pp. 3 et seq. *Information on the activities of the Ombudsman in 2009 and the state of observance of human and civil liberties and rights*, Wydawnictwo RPO, Warsaw 2010.

be emphasized, however, that they were related to the efforts of the Ombudsman to prevent the creation of another government special administration, but to make it a competence of local government, in accordance with the constitutional principle of subsidiarity.

The poviat is able – in terms of content and personnel – to organize free legal aid. This is the satisfaction of the collective needs of the inhabitants, so it should be – in line with the subsidiarity principle – the poviat's own task, because in the case of smaller communes it exceeds the management span.

The Ombudsman in Poland, almost from the beginning of the establishment of the office (1988), sought to increase legal awareness among citizens and to create the basis for free legal aid[4]. The issues of increasing legal awareness and free legal aid were often combined with each other as similar elements of legal and civic education[5]. In addition to the Ombudsman's activities constantly raising the legal awareness of citizens by organizing and participating in numerous meetings, conferences, running his own website with free access to guidance materials, etc., the Defender played a significant role in creating free legal aid, acting as an entity that gave a normative impulse also by raising the voice of stakeholders cooperating with him to the rank of general speeches.

However, the first fully verbalized attempts to create a framework for free legal aid were associated with the necessity to prostheses the system of professional legal aid provided by representatives of the legal professions, mainly advocates and legal advisers. This system was also supported by the work of its officials from the beginning of the establishment of the Human Rights Defender's Office. In this regard, a significant number of new applications filed with the ROP should be indicated, amounting to as much as 35,000. in 2013[6] and the general statement that "the Defender is treated as the proverbial" last resort "not only in cases where the clients have exhausted all legal measures to protect their rights, but also in a situation where the answer obtained ex officio was formulated contrary to their expectations or when such a response was not understood"[7].

The analysis of the annual information of the Commissioner for Human Rights shows that the first form of the indicated "prosthesis" was legal counseling provided by university legal clinics, law clinics, i.e., units organized at law faculties,

4 T. Zieliński, *for the period from February 13, 1993 to February 12,* 1994, „Biuletyn RPO", Warszawa 1994, p. 31. Cf. E. Łętowska, *Baba na świeczniku,* Warszawa 1992.

5 See e.g. Information of the Ombudsman prof. Andrzej Zoll for the year 2000, Warsaw 2001, p. 293; Information of the Ombudsman, prof. Andrzej Zoll for 2001, Warsaw 2002, pp. 10 and 11; Information of the Ombudsman for 2005, Warsaw 2006, pp. 258–260.

6 B. Przywora, *Normatywny model przedsądowej nieodpłatnej pomocy prawnej w Polsce,* Warszawa 2019.

7 Information of the Ombudsman prof. Andrzej Zoll for 2000, Warszawa 2001, pp. 291–292.

in which students, under the supervision of professional lawyers, provided legal advice to the poor[8]. From the very beginning, however, it was not about creating competition for services provided on the legal market, but supplementing the possibility of using legal advice to protect their rights and freedoms by indigent people, for whom the market prices of legal services prevented professional service at the pre-trial stage. The lack of a systemic solution for free legal advice infringed the basic principle expressed in art. 45 of the Constitution RP – the right to a fair trial[9]. Of course, it was not about its general exclusion, but about the consequences of ignorance about the possibility of exercising this right and the rules on which it should be exercised. Interestingly, the representatives of the Ministry of Justice generally shared the ills of the legal services system in Poland, noticed by the Ombudsman, and the important role of "University Legal Clinics, as playing a significant role in providing free legal advice to people whose financial situation does not allow them to benefit from this type of assistance"[10].

The functioning of the University Legal Clinics was of particular concern to the Ombudsman. The Ombudsman, apart from concluding agreements with counseling centers and an important but symbolic gesture, in the form of awarding a prize to one of the civic counseling offices[11] "for consistency in activities to build a civil society by raising the legal and civic awareness of the local community", he was also involved in providing legal counselors with fuller access to court files in criminal cases. This indicated the importance attached to this type of legal aid by the Ombudsman[12].

The real breakthrough came when the Ombudsman took the initiative[13] to organize a debate initiating work on the preparation of a systemic statutory solution regulating free legal aid in Poland. As a result of the Defender's work preceded by a general appeal to the Minister of Justice in this matter[14], on 6 October 2004, the "Access to information and legal advice – system solutions" conference was held at the Human Rights Defender's Office. It resulted in recommendations for

8 Information of the Ombudsman prof. Andrzej Zoll for 2003, Warszawa 2004, p. 7; Information of the Ombudsman prof. Andrzej Zoll for 2003, Warszawa 2004, pp. 362–363.

9 Information on the activities of the Human Rights Defender in 2009 and on the state of observance of human and civil liberties and rights, Warsaw 2010, p. 72.

10 Information of the Ombudsman prof. Andrzej Zoll for 2003, Warszawa 2004, pp. 362–363.

11 Information of the Ombudsman for 2005, Warszawa 2006, pp. 258–260.

12 Information of the Ombudsman prof. Andrzej Zoll for 2003, Warszawa 2004, pp. 362–363.

13 The Ombudsman was approached by: the Foundation of University Legal Clinics, the Helsinki Foundation for Human Rights, the Polish Association of Legal Education, the Union of Citizens Advice Bureaus.

14 Letter of the Ombudsman of August 3, 2004, ref. No. 481256-IV-04 and a positive answer of the Minister of Justice of September 13, 2004, ref. No. P.II. 4308/727/04.

the creation of the act[15] and the appointment in the Ministry of Justice of a team for the preparation of a draft law on access to free legal aid granted by the state to natural persons, the work of which culminated in the submission to the Sejm of the Republic of Poland on 23 March 2005 (Sejm form 3838/4th term of the Sejm)[16].

The role of the Ombudsman in initiating work on the act has – which is rare – explicitly stated in the justification to the draft act. It stated that: "the need to introduce solutions enabling the poor people to access legal aid was repeatedly pointed out by the Ombudsman, asking the Minister of Justice to initiate legislative work in this area. The Ombudsman argued that the standards set by the Constitution RP and Poland's international obligations in the field of the implementation of human rights and freedoms require the creation of a system of legal protection"[17]. The prospect of sorting out this issue has come closer.

Unfortunately, with the end of the 4th term of the Sejm (2005) and the change of the political majority, the legislative process over this legal act came to a halt. The Ombudsman also undertook numerous interventions in this regard, including those of a substantive nature[18]. The words of Janusz Kochanowski, who said: "In 2009, the Ombudsman once again addressed the issue of regulating access to free legal aid for the poor. In this case, the Ombudsman has been corresponding with the Minister of Justice for over five years, each time pointing to the absolute necessity to create a new, coherent, transparent, and fair system that would guarantee the effective use of the constitutional right to a fair trial to all citizens, regardless of their level of wealth. Although in the common opinion – also shared by successive governments, regardless of their political options – the above issue has always been a priority, for years it cannot be properly regulated, which raises serious concerns"[19]. In 2013, another Ombudsman alerted in the annual report that the lack of functioning of the universal system of legal aid and legal information means that the Office of the Ombudsman is treated by citizens not as an entity protecting their rights, but as a place of obtaining information on how and where they should settle their matters. It is theoretically interesting: Due to the inactivity of the authorities, a syndrome of "orphaned competencies" arises in a socially

---

15 Report from the conference and the text of the proposed solutions: https://www.fupp.org.pl/kliniki-prawa/konferencje/9-polski/aktualnosci/26-seminarium-rpo-2004 (accessed: 3.03.2021).

16 Information of the Ombudsman for 2004, Warszawa 2005, pp. 331–332, 350.

17 Justification to the bill, Sejm Print 3838/IV term of Sejm, p. 1.

18 Information of the Ombudsman for 2006, Warszawa 2007, pp. 40–41; Information on the activities of the Ombudsman in 2008 and on the state of observance of human and civil freedoms and rights, Warsaw 2009, pp. 81–82; Information on the activities of the Ombudsman in 2009 and on the state of observance of human and civic freedoms and rights, Warsaw 2010, p. 72; Information of the Ombudsman for 2012, Warsaw 2013.

19 Information on the activities of the Ombudsman in 2009 and on the state of observance of human and civil liberties and rights, Warsaw 2010, p. 72.

important area. Competences cannot be "traded" and transferred to another body. This gap was partially filled by non-governmental organizations and their voluntary involvement, partially by expanding the activities of the ROP within its original competences and under pressure from stakeholders.

The lack of significant work on subsequent bills (Sejm's form on 29 May 2/each parliamentary term and 29 May/Mayor of the Sejm – an auto-amendment significantly changing the previous draft) as well as the lack of proceeding with new bills in 2007–2011 (sixth term of the Sejm) allows for conclusions that the freeze of works was not of a political nature[20]. The years 2007–2011 saw the repetition of the Ombudsman's addresses to the Minister of Justice constantly indicating the need to undertake legislative work. In response, the ministry informed about "ongoing work on the bill". It is clear that the deeply justified legislative proposals of the Ombudsman have been ignored for a long time.

The Ombudsman Irena Lipowicz in a parliamentary speech in 2012 stated, inter alia, that 18 thousand. of the previous year's cases was in fact seeking free legal aid. She spoke out against the construction of a parallel "superadministration" of legal aid for the system of dispersed, multi-entity, publicly financed[21]. All the time seeking to release the act, during the 2010–2015 term of office, certain substitute activities were carried out, i.e., receiving citizens in cities where there were no local Ombudsman's Offices (Lublin, Olsztyn) and coordination activities for various helplines, as well as the creation of a free Ombudsman hotline. operated by substantive specialists, not only people accepting applications.

A significant breakthrough in the field of adopting new legal solutions took place only with the commencement of work on the draft of 16 April 2015 on the law on free legal aid, free legal information, and legal education of the society (Sejm paper no. 3338/VII term of the Sejm). Although it was brought to the marshal's staff in the last year of the Sejm's operation in the 7th term, it was adopted on 5 August 2015.

---

20 In the annual report for 2006 (Warsaw 2007), the Ombudsman indicated: "The Minister of Justice informed that the issue of legal aid, including free assistance for the poor, remains in the sphere of interest of the Government, and in particular of the Minister of Justice. There is a need to improve and extend the scope of legal aid, especially for the poor, but the draft law on access to free legal aid granted by the state to natural persons, which was submitted by the previous Government, requires serious adjustments. The Minister of Justice asked the Marshal of the Sejm of the Republic of Poland to postpone work on this draft until the solutions provided for in it were refined, and, as a consequence, the self-amendment prepared by the Council of Ministers was submitted. The development of the Government's self-amendment requires many actions and analyzes. The draft budget for 2006 does not provide for funds to finance expenditure resulting from the entry into force of the draft act. Hence, there is a need to provide financial resources in the state budget for the implementation of this task. Another broad consultation with law corporations and other institutions and non-governmental organizations will be necessary", p. 41.

21 I. Lipowicz, *O mądre i wrażliwe państwo*, Warszawa 2013, pp. 314–315, pp. 199–200.

The justification indicated that the project was the implementation of the political demands signaled on 1 October 2014 in the exposé of the Prime Minister, as well as the implementation of the country's development strategy until 2020[22]. The impact assessment of the regulation indicated, however, that the proposed act is to solve the problem of insufficient legal awareness of citizens raised by the Ombudsman and an underdeveloped broadly understood legal culture. This is another argument for a strong participation of the Ombudsman in the process leading to the creation of the right to free legal aid in Poland, but participation in the conditions of no legislative initiative. The Ombudsman may not also cause the submission of a bill by a Parliamentary Club or a party due to the obligation of impartiality.

It should be noted that the Ombudsman interest in the act did not end with its adoption. And although, for natural reasons, the cases of free legal aid are no longer the main element of the Defender's endeavors, he remains the body that carefully assesses the functioning of the right to free legal aid. In this regard, the Ombudsman pointed to the lack of implementing provisions to the Act specifying the rules for selecting non-governmental organizations to run free legal counseling points[23] or concluded that despite the existence of free assistance, "the Office of the Ombudsman is sometimes mistakenly treated as an entity providing free legal aid". It often happens those citizens – dissatisfied with the quality of assistance provided by free legal counseling centers – expect complementary support from the Ombudsman. The Ombudsman, however, saw the basis of the emerging problems in the poor quality of law, and not in the existence of a clinic[24].

The currently binding act is critically assessed in the doctrine[25]. In particular, its drawback is the limitation of the possibility of drawing up pleadings in connection with, inter alia, with the erroneous assumption that ex officio attorney-in-fact admission is common. Indirectly, it is possible to infer its ineffectiveness due to the lack of a significant decrease in the inflow of cases to the Ombudsman despite the lapse of five years from the entry into force of the Act. Even taking into account the general deterioration in the quality of administration in recent years in the re-centralized areas, the decrease in the number of applications in fact seeking legal aid should be significant. In the Ombudsman's report from 2019, such a decrease was not recorded.

From the above considerations, a conclusion can be drawn that the Ombudsman actively pursues the issuance and then the necessary amendment to the law on free

---

22 Resolution No. 157 of the Council of Ministers of 25 September 2012 on the adoption of the National Development Strategy 2020 (Polish Ministry of Finance of 2012, item 882).

23 Information on the activities of the Ombudsman for 2018 and the state of observance of human and civil liberties and rights, Warsaw 2019, p. 148.

24 Information on the activities of the Ombudsman for 2019 and the state of observance of human and civil freedoms and rights, Warsaw 2020, p. 475.

25 B. Przywora, *op. cit.*, passim.

legal aid in accordance with the postulates presented in the doctrine. Ombudsmen consistently return to these postulates in annual reports and public appearances.

In the light of these de lege ferenda experiences, a conclusion can be drawn that Parliamentary Clubs would have to obligatorily and in writing respond to the Ombudsman's conclusions expressed in the annual information, including applications for free legal aid. However, in order to ensure the independence of the Ombudsman, the lack of the possibility to vote on accepting or rejecting the annual report of the Ombudsman. Additional positive social pressure on the implementation of these requests could be ensured by the legally regulated enforcement of the mission of public television and public radio in such a way as to ensure direct transmission of the annual information of the Ombudsman, and the Sejm's regulations should guarantee the hours of presenting this information in the so-called prime time – prime time. Part of the implementation of this mission would be the right of the Ombudsman to an annual public television speech on World Human Rights Day on 8 December, as do the Speakers of the Sejm and Senate.

A paradigm shift in the field of legal aid which reduces the need for giving free help to embrace sizes should become a universal law and insurance mediation, partly subsidized by the state, also postulated in the past by the Ombudsman.

In the discussion on free legal aid, the role of the Ombudsman leads to more general conclusions. Firstly – the existence and active operation of the Ombudsman institution is not able, as indicated, to replace the system of free legal aid and information. Secondly, however, the existence of a strong institution of this type was part of a long-lasting but ultimately effective pressure to create a system of legal aid for people in need. Thirdly, the system in place since 2015 still contains disturbing dysfunctions in the scope of assistance. Certain categories of vulnerable persons require special legal aid, e.g., victims of crimes deprived in practice of a defective and complicated procedure of compensation due to them under European law.

However, even removing the main errors will be an action only within the existing system in which we agree in advance with the inconsistent, incomprehensible, poor-quality law, and we focus only on its limited explanation to the poor. The allocation of public funds should also concern, to a greater extent, the improvement of the quality of legislation.

Some of the "substitute" legal aid measures taken by the Ombudsman in the absence of a relevant act should remain permanent. These include, for example, cooperation with civic and university counseling centers, as well as training and coordination of the staff of social helplines, which also provide information and legal aid, e.g., for abused children, people with depression or addictions.

Literature

Łętowska E., *Baba na świeczniku*, Warszawa 1992.

Przywora B., *Normatywny model przedsądowej nieodpłatnej pomocy prawnej w Polsce*, Warszawa 2019.

Zieliński A., *Wielkość prawa budujemy wszyscy*, Warszawa 2000.

Zieliński T., *Sprawozdanie RPO za okres od 13 lutego 1993 r. do 12 lutego 1994 r.*, „Biuletyn RPO", Warszawa 1994.

Zoll A., *Państwo prawa jeszcze w budowie*, Warszawa 2013.

Piotr Ruczkowski[1] and Leszek Bielecki[2]

The issue of free prejudicial legal aid and the principle of the right to a fair trial

Abstract: The study aims to analyze the issue of free legal aid in the context of the principle of the right to a fair trial. The aim of the paper will be to confirm the hypothesis where the possibility of using free legal aid, in the case of economically vulnerable people, forms one of the premises for putting into effect the principle of the right to a fair trial, and in particular where it extends the scope of access to court. According to the initial assumption, the possibility of using free legal aid should also be considered in the context of the principle of a democratic state ruled by law, or the *rule of law*, the principle of justice, principles of equality before the law, principles of trust in the state and law, principles of legal security and legal certainty.

Keywords: free legal aid, the right to a fair trial, legal security

1. Introduction

The subject of the study is the analysis of problems of free legal aid at the pretrial stage and legal assistance (the right to legal assistance) in a trial based on the principle of the right to a fair trial. The considerations brought forward in this elaboration will represent a continuation and development of research on the issue of legal aid in Polish and European law conducted in the doctrine[3].

This paper will aim to support the hypothesis, which assumes that the possibility of using free legal aid at the pretrial stage and the institution of legal aid (the

---

1 Jan Kochanowski University, Kielce. ORCID: 0000-0003-4344-9417.
2 Jan Kochanowski University, Kielce. ORCID: 0000-0002-1553-1141.
3 See articles on this topic: M. Jabłoński, *Prawo do nieodpłatnej pomocy prawnej jako „element treści konstytucyjnego prawa do sądu" – uwagi na te postanowień ustawy z 5 sierpnia 2015 r. o nieodpłatnej pomocy prawnej oraz edukacji prawnej*, [in:] A. Hauser, M. Urbaniak (eds.), *Ochrona praw człowieka. Zagadnienia praktyczne*, Poznań 2019; S. Trociuk, *Pomoc prawna dla osób ubogich jako forma zapewnienia skutecznego dostępu do krajowego i europejskiego wymiaru sprawiedliwości*, [in:] H. Izdebski, H. Machińska (eds.), *Dostęp obywateli do europejskiego wymiaru sprawiedliwości*, Warszawa 2005.

right to legal assistance) in court and administrative court proceedings, in the case of persons in financial difficulty, belong to the premises of putting into effect the principle of the right to a fair trial, in particular, they extend the scope of equal access to justice, are part of the rights of defence and a feature of a fair trial. Failing to provide legal aid may violate the above-mentioned principles guaranteeing citizens the right to a fair hearing by impartial and independent courts.

The right to a fair trial, including the rights of defence and the principle of procedural fairness, can be derived from the general clause of a democratic state of law that implements the principles of social justice and the resulting standards of a democratic state. Hence, the possibility of benefiting from free legal aid at the pretrial phase and the right to legal aid in court proceedings can be examined in the context of the values of a democratic and law-abiding state (in particular the concept of the *rule of law*; principles: justice, equality before the law, trust in the state and law, protection of acquired rights, legal security and legal certainty).

At this point, it is worth stressing that the right to free legal aid applies not only to court proceedings, but also to proceedings before public administration bodies, but due to the adopted scope of research, determined by the title of the study, this topic will be omitted.

As already mentioned above, in accordance with the adopted methodological assumptions, the subject of the analysis shall first and foremost be free legal aid at the pretrial stage, whereas to a slightly limited extent due to the limited volume of the study, it will also concern legal aid in civil and criminal proceedings and the right to assistance in administrative court proceedings covering full or partial exemption from costs related to the proceedings as well as the appointment of an attorney (counselor, legal advisor), tax advisor or patent attorney. Already at this stage of work, it must be emphasized that those are separate regulations provided primarily by procedural law and that they certainly serve to grant real access to court. They are examples of the implementation of the guarantee function of law as one of the components (procedural guarantees) of the idea of procedural justice.

The dogmatic nature of the paper implies the selection and use of research tools and methods. Amongst the applied research methods, the dominant one is the dogmatic (analytical-dogmatic) approach, the essence of which is the exegesis of a legal text using linguistic and non-linguistic rules for interpreting the law.

In view of the adopted research assumptions, the historical method and the comparative law method were omitted.

2. Free legal aid and the right to legal aid in the light of universal and regional systems of human rights protection and EU law

As signalized in the introductory comments to this elaboration, the right to legal aid in the pretrial phase and during the pending proceedings can be considered in the context of the principle of the right to a fair trial, or more specifically as one of the conditions for broadening the extent of access to judicial protection of individual freedoms and rights in a democratic state ruled by law, one of the assumptions of which is the implementation of the principle of social justice and the principle of equality, including the equalization of opportunities for people in financial or social difficulty in access to the justice system.

The right to a fair trial fulfills a special, fundamental guarantee role in the sphere of protection of the freedoms and rights of an individual, therefore it has been guaranteed in the universal and regional systems of human rights protection.

The right to a fair trial (judicial protection of individual freedoms and rights) is guaranteed by the provisions of, for example, the United Nations Universal Declaration of Human Rights of 10 December 1948[4] (art. 8; art. 10), the International Covenant on Civil and Political Rights of 9 December 1966 (art. 2; art. 14 (1)), as well as the ECHR of 4 November 1950[5] (art. 6 (1)).

As with the abovementioned international documents, the principle of the right to a fair trial is expressed directly or indirectly (it can be derived from the principle of democratism, the rule of law, protection of individual freedoms and fundamental rights) in legal acts of the EU, especially in the content of the TEU and the TFEU, the provisions of the CFR, which, due to the entry into force of the Treaty of Lisbon, obtained the status of primary EU law, as well as the Code of Good Administrative Behavior proclaimed by the European Parliament on 6 September 2001[6] (ECHA) and Recommendation of the Committee of Ministers of the Council of Europe of 20 June 2007 – *Right to Good Administration.* It is worth pointing out that in this case, it is not just about the right to a fair trial at the EU (in particular the right to access the Court of Justice of the European Union – CJEU), but also – through the principles of primacy, the direct effect and direct applicability of EU law – the right to judicial protection of freedoms and rights guaranteed by this law by the national courts of the Member States.

The cited regulations will guarantee everyone, including foreigners, the right to a fair and public hearing by competent, impartial, and independent courts.

The right to a fair trial means not only guaranteeing broad access to a fair trial, i.e., a public authority characterized by impartiality and judicial independence, the proper conduct of the trial and the swift and effective execution of judicial decisions, but also a number of other procedural guarantees aimed at an equitable outcome of the proceedings, which are constituents of the principle of procedural fairness[7]. Not without reason, the literature emphasizes that the principle of the right to a fair trial is closely connected (linked) with the principle of procedural fairness[8]. That said, at this point it is worth stressing that the principle of

---

4 Journal of Laws of 1993, No. 61, item 284.
5 EU Journal od Laws 2011/C 285/3.
6 Judgment of the ECtHR of 22 March 2012 in case 19508/07 (Granos Organicos Nacionales S.A. v Germany), LEX No. 1130584.
7 J. Zimmermann, *Prawo administracyjne*, Warszawa 2016, p. 164.
8 Ibidem, p 164.

procedural fairness applies not only to proceedings before a court, but also to those conducted by public administration bodies, especially jurisdictional administrative proceedings (general proceedings), and therefore it is often distinguished and analyzed alongside the principle of the right to a fair trial[9].

The principle of procedural fairness can also be derived from the idea of a democratic state of law. It does not apply to a single legal institution since it contains a system of procedural guarantees (the values of the proceedings) aimed at ensuring the correct and fair course of a court trial or administrative procedure[10]. Amongst the mentioned procedural guarantees, we should also list the right to using legal aid at every stage of the proceedings, including the stage prior to the initiation of the proceeding, namely preparation for trial.

The significance of the right to legal aid for the implementation of the rule of the right to a fair trial resulting from art. 6 of the ECHR was brought forward by the ECtHR in its judgment of 13 March 2007 in case no. 77765/01 of *Laskowska v. Polska*, Chamber (Section IV)[11], where it was argued that failure to provide the assistance of a counselor may lead to a violation of the right to a fair trial, especially when legal representation is obligatory; this is justified by the complexity of the proceedings or the type of case. Without a doubt, the lack of access to free legal aid in the case of people in a difficult financial or social situation may lead to a restriction or even total deprivation of access to a fair trial, and thus may deprive of judicial protection of violated rights or freedoms. This is especially relevant in the context of criminal and administrative court proceedings, which involves the risk of a severe sanction and the legality of the usually authoritative actions of public administration in relation to administered entities is controlled. In this context, it is worth noting art. 6 (3) lit. c, which *explicite* guarantees the right of the accused to use a defense counsel, and in the event of insufficient financial resources, the right to free assistance of a defense lawyer by the State.

In the light of this, it is important to note that the right to a fair trial, one aspect of which is represented by the right of access to legal aid, is not absolute but may be subject to restrictions. Nonetheless, the applied restrictions cannot limit nor diminish the access left to individuals in such a way or to such an extent that the very essence of that right is violated. Restricting access to court will not be compatible with art. 6 (1) of the ECHR, if it does not pursue a legitimate aim and if there is no reasonable relationship of proportionality between the means used and the object to be achieved. The ECHR does not impose the obligation to provide [ex

9 E. Olejniczak-Szałowska, *Zasada sprawiedliwości proceduralnej*, [in:] M. Stahl (ed.), *Prawo administracyjne. Pojęcia, instytucje, zasady w teorii i orzecznictwie*, Warszawa 2016, pp. 175–176.

10 Z. Kmieciak, *Idea sprawiedliwości proceduralnej w prawie administracyjnym (Założenia teoretyczne i doświadczenia praktyki)*, „Państwo i Prawo" 1994, z. 10, p. 55 et seq.

11 M. A. Nowicki, *Europejski Trybunał Praw Człowieka. Wybór orzeczeń 2007*, Warszawa 2008, p. 30.

officio] legal aid for all disputes in civil proceedings, as there is a clear differentiation between the wording of art. 6 (3) lit. c of the ECHR, which guarantees the right to obtain free legal aid under certain conditions in criminal proceedings, and art. 6 (1) of the ECHR, which does not refer to legal aid at all. It is important to note that the right of access to courts is not absolute and may be limited, in particular, to preserve legitimate grounds for controlling the use of public funds to finance private litigation. When a person's access to court is limited due to an applicable legal provision or by a factual restriction, such a restriction will not be incompatible with art. 6 when it does not infringe the very essence of this right and pursues a legitimate aim, and also when there is a reasonable relationship of proportionality between the means used and the aim to be [thus] achieved[12].

The right to benefit from free legal aid in the event of a difficult financial situation is provided for in art. 14 (3) point d of the above-mentioned International Covenant on Civil and Political Rights.

Among other normative acts that require the need to provide legal assistance is the so-called Istanbul Convention, i.e., the Council of Europe Convention on preventing and combating violence against women and domestic violence, drawn up in Istanbul on 11 May 2011[13]. Art. 20 of the Convention provides for the obligation of the parties to pursue necessary measures whose aim will be to provide victims of violence with, inter alia, institutionalized legal aid.

The right to a fair trial, including the right to legal aid, was explicitly *guaranteed,* and included among the fundamental rights in art. 47 of the CFR. Under that provision, all persons whose rights and freedoms guaranteed by Union law are violated are entitled to an effective remedy before a tribunal in compliance with the conditions laid down in this article. Everyone is entitled to a fair and public hearing within a reasonable time by an independent and impartial tribunal previously established by law. Everyone has the opportunity to obtain legal advice, use the help of a defense lawyer and representative. Legal help is provided to people to the extent in which they do not have sufficient resources insofar as it is necessary to ensure effective access to justice.

Moreover, in art. 48 sec. 2 of the CFR, the accused was guaranteed respect for the rights of defence.

It is worth stressing that legal aid is the subject of EU secondary legislation. In this respect, it is worth paying attention to Council Directive 2003/8/EC of 27 January 2003 on improving access to justice in cross-border disputes[14], the effect of which is to guarantee legal aid to a party who resides or is continuously present in a Member State other than that in which the court is situated or in which the judgment is to be enforced and who is wholly or partially unable to bear the costs of the trial owing to their economic situation. This help serves to ensure efficient

12 Journal of Laws of 2020, item 30.
13 Decision of the Supreme Court of 17 July 2014 in case V KZ 26/14, LEX No. 1487098.
14 EU Journal of Laws 2003/L 026.

access to justice and involves (a) pretrial advice, in order to settle a dispute before bringing the matter to court, and (b) legal aid and representation in court, exemption of legal aid from legal costs or assistance in paying these costs, as well as related to the renumeration of persons authorized by the court to perform activities during trial.

At this point, it is important to emphasize that a number of EU provisions that provide for free legal assistance applies to foreigners, especially to persons applying for refugee status or another form of international protection, e.g. Directive 2013/32/EU of the European Parliament and of the Council of 26 June 2013 on common procedures for granting and withdrawing international protection (recast)[15] and Directive 2013/33/EU of the European Parliament and of the Council of 26 June 2013 laying down standards for the reception of applicants for international protection[16].

The right to a fair trial and the right to legal aid are regulated by the Council of Europe in the scope of the so-called soft law. In this context, attention should be paid, inter alia, to Recommendation No. R (93) of the Committee of the Council of Ministers of the Council of Europe to member states on effective access to law and justice for the poorest[17].

3. Free legal aid and the right to legal aid in court proceedings under national law

To depart to national law, it should be noted that the right to a fair trial is not only an element expressed in art. 2 of the Constitution RP of the principle of a democratic state of law that implements the rules of social justice and the resulting standards of a democratic state (the concept of the *rule of law*; principles: justice, equality before the law, trust in the state and law, protection of acquired rights, legal security and legal certainty), but is also separately formulated in a number of its provisions, including art. 45 (1), art. 77 (2) and in art. 184[18].

In the jurisprudence of the Constitutional Tribunal, attention is drawn to the structural elements of the right to a fair trial, namely it is emphasized that "The constitutional right to a fair trial consists in particular of: (1) the right of access to court, i.e. the right to initiate a procedure before a court – an authority with

15 Journal of Laws of 2019, item 2325.

16 Decision of the Provincial Administrative Court in Lublin of 19 November 2018 in case II SA/Lu 461/18.

17 See M. Kaczocha, *Ustawa o nieodpłatnej pomocy prawnej i edukacji prawnej*, LEX/el. 2016; B. Przywora, A. Wróbel, *Poradnictwo obywatelskie w świetle badań prawnoporównawczych*, Warszawa 2020, p. 28.

18 The judgments of the CT of 7 January 1992, K 8/91, OTK no. 1/1991, item 5; 27 January 1999, K 1/98, OTK no. 1/1999, item 3; 14 June 1999, K 11/98, OTK 1999, No. 5, item 97.

specific characteristics (impartial and independent); (2) the right to an appropriate shaping of the court procedure in accordance with the requirements of justice and openness; (3) the right to a court judgment, i.e. the right to obtain a binding decision of a given case by a court"[19].

The Constitutional Tribunal emphasizes that "The place of art. 45 in the systematics of the Constitution indicates the autonomous nature of the right to a fair trial. It is not merely an instrument enabling the exercise of other constitutional rights and freedoms, but it has its own imperative and is subject to protection irrespective of the violation of other subjective rights. The constitutional formula of the right to a fair trial also has another meaning; it is a principle of constitutional law and in this sense a law-making directive and an interpretative directive"[20].

As we recall, also the principle of procedural fairness can be derived from the idea of a democratic state ruled by law, which is confirmed by the judicature of the courts. For example, the Supreme Administrative Court stated in its judgment of 19 October 1993 that "The right to a fair procedure, due to its significant importance in the process of realizing civil rights and freedoms, falls within the content of the rule of law[21]"

It is worth mentioning that traditional institutions aimed at ensuring the actual implementation of the right to court include legal assistance in civil and criminal proceedings or the right to assistance in administrative court proceedings, consisting in the possibility of exemption from costs related to the proceedings, as well as the appointment of a counselor, attorney-at-law, tax advisor or patent attorney acting as a representative. Such solutions are provided for in each proceeding, including administrative court proceedings, and generally apply to persons who, due to their difficult financial situation, are not in a position to bear the costs related to the proceedings.

In the context of today's Polish legal system, only court proceedings guarantee the possibility of obtaining free legal aid for persons who do not have sufficient funds to cover the costs of representation by a counselor or legal advisor.

In civil proceedings, the granting of legal aid is governed by the provisions of art. 117–124 of the Act of 17 November 1964 – Code of Civil Procedure[22]. The court may grant the assistance of a counselor or legal advisor, if the party, by providing

---

19 The judgment of the CT of 9 June 1998, K 28/97, OTK ZU no. 4/1998, item 50.

20 The judgment of the CT of 13 May 2002, SK 32/01, OTK ZU no. 3/A/2002, item 31.

21 The judgment of the Supreme Administrative Court of 19 October 1993, V SA 250/93, OSP 1995, No. 5, item 101.

22 *Journal of Laws 2023*, item 1550.

detailed data on the family status, property, income, and sources of income, will prove that he is not able to incur the costs of a counselor's or legal advisor's remuneration without prejudice to his and his family's subsistence. The prerequisite for appointing a counselor (legal advisor) for a party not released by the court from legal costs is to prove that he cannot, without prejudice to his and his family's subsistence (which means the possibility of maintenance at the level of members of a family with average earnings), bear the costs of the remuneration of an attorney[23].

In criminal proceedings, an accused who does not have an elected defense lawyer may – under art. 78 § 1 of the Act of 6 June 1997 – Code of Criminal Procedure (CCP)[24] – demand that an ex officio defender be appointed, if he duly proves that he is unable to bear the costs of defense without prejudice to ability to arrange his own or family members' maintenance. The wording of art. 78 § 1 of the Code of Criminal Procedure urges to demonstrate that one is unable to meet the costs of one's defense without compromising the necessary subsistence for their or family members' maintenance. Therefore, the property of the convict at the time of submitting the application for the appointment of a public defender is examined, and not a hypothetical assumption. The appointment of a public defender should therefore take place both in a situation where the convicted person does not have sufficient means to cover the costs of defense of his choice and when the resources are so scarce that they do not allow to cover these costs and provide the necessary subsistence for their or family members' maintenance at the basic level. It cannot be assumed that the determinant of this financial situation is the "hidden" source of income of the convict and his potential earning opportunities[25]. It should also be noted that depriving the accused of a justified right to choose a defense counsel, also by refusing to appoint that counsel under art. 78 § 1 of the CCP, may in principle affect the wording of the judgment. This applies especially to cases where the facts relevant to the determination of guilt are determined on the basis of the assessment of contradictory evidence. Pursuant to art. 88 of the Code of Criminal Procedure, this regulation applies accordingly to the appointment of an attorney for a party other than the accused and for a person who is not a party.

In court and administrative proceedings, the right to obtain the assistance of a professional attorney is covered by the Assistance Law, regulated in art. 243–263 of the Act of 30 August 2002 – Law on proceedings before administrative courts[26]. The right to assistance is granted only in connection with proceedings before an administrative court, if a party can prove that he is unable to bear any of the costs of the proceedings or the full costs of the proceedings, without prejudice to the subsistence necessary for himself and his family. Determining whether there is

---

23 The decision of the Court of Appeal in Rzeszów of 18 January 2013, III AUz 3/13, LEX no. 1264434.

24 Journal of Laws of 2022, item 1375)

25 The Supreme Court's decision of 17 July 2014, V KZ 26/14, LEX no. 1487098.

26 *Journal of Laws of 2023*, item 1634.

a prerequisite for granting partial aid requires a comparison of the current financial capacity of the party applying for the aid to the amount of costs that it must incur during the procedure, considering the amount of the fixed maintenance costs as required. The funds remaining after the costs of the proceedings have been incurred must make it possible to cover the expenses related to the necessary maintenance costs of the party applying for the aid and its family[27].

Likewise, the Act of 28 July 2005 on Judicial Costs in Civil Cases[28] (u.k.s.c.) provides for partial exemption from legal costs if the party can bear only part of these costs. The institution of exemption from paying court fees is, in fact, state aid for people who, due to their particularly difficult financial situation, cannot bear these costs without prejudice to the maintenance necessary for themselves and their family, especially the unemployed, sick, lonely, without a stable source of income and without property where dismissal of the application for an exemption would infringe their right to a fair trial[29]. On the other hand, temporary financial difficulties do not exhaust the premises covered by art. 101 para. 1 in connection with art. 102 para1 u.k.s.c.[30] Exemptions from paying court fees may be requested by a natural person, if he or she submits a declaration that proves that he or she is unable to bear these costs without prejudice to the maintenance necessary for himself and his family or incurring them will expose him to such damage. Pursuant to 102 sec. 1 and 2 of u.k.s.c., the party claiming exemption from legal costs is obliged to prove in the submitted declaration that paying the required fee would result in a detriment to the necessary support for himself and his family. These circumstances require examination (determination and assessment) by the court competent to give an effective decision on the application[31]. That said, it should be noted that the exemption from legal costs does not release the party from the obligation to reimburse the legal costs of the opponent.

On the other hand, an autonomous institution, although at least partially pursuing similar goals, is free legal aid at the pretrial stage, regulated by the Free Legal Aid Act. As outlined in the explanatory memorandum accompanying the bill, it "gives substance of the country's development strategy until 2020, set out in the Resolution No. 157 of the Council of Ministers of 25 September 2012 on the adoption of the National Development Strategy 2020 (MP of 2012, item 882), which provides for better access to legal information and legal services, including access to legal aid for people in difficult life situations which they cannot overcome using their own powers, resources and possibilities". The legislator therefore holds that although a number of public institutions, parliamentarians' offices,

27 Decision of Administrative Court in Lublin of 19 November 2018, II SA/Lu 461/18.

28 *Journal of Laws of 2023*, item 1144.

29 Decision of the Supreme Court of 23 January 2019 in the case I CZ 1/19, LEX No. 2618545.

30 Decision of the Supreme Court of 17 April 2015, I CZ 35/15, LEX no. 1712804.

31 Decision of the Supreme Court of 11 September 2020 in the case I CZ 45/20, LEX No. 3071513.

non-governmental organizations and other entities provide – apart from their core tasks – legal assistance, it is necessary to establish such organizational and legal solutions, the main purpose and direction of which will be to provide citizens whose financial status does not allow to cover the costs of legal advice on the free market, with access to legal aid at the pretrial stage, whereby it is intended to be provided by a professional (counselor, legal advisor, etc.).

According to the act in question, free legal assistance includes: (1) informing a natural person about the applicable legal status and his/her rights or obligations, including in connection with pending preparatory, administrative, court or administrative court proceedings; (2) indicating to the entitled person the method of solving his legal problem or (3) drawing up a draft letter in the matters referred to in points 1 and 2, with the exception of pleadings in pending preparatory or court proceedings and letters in pending administrative court proceedings, or (4) free mediation, or (5) drawing up a draft letter for exemption from paying court fees or appointing an ex officio attorney in court proceedings or appointing a counselor, legal advisor, tax advisor or patent attorney in administrative court proceedings and informing about the costs of the proceedings and the financial risk related to bringing the case to court. On the other hand, free-of-charge civic counseling includes activities tailored to the individual circumstances of the entitled person, aimed at raising the awareness of that person in relation to their rights or obligations and supporting them in independent problem-solving, including, if necessary, drawing up an action plan together with the entitled person and helping in its implementation. Free-of-charge civic counseling includes in particular advice for indebted persons and advice on housing and social security matters. Free-of-charge civic counseling also includes free mediation. In turn, legal education involves educational activities which serve to increase the society's legal awareness regarding spreading knowledge on (1) civil rights and obligations; (2) activities of national and international legal protection bodies; (3) mediation and methods of amicable dispute resolution; (4) opportunities for citizens to participate in public consultations and the law-making process; (5) access to free legal aid and free-of-charge civic counseling. All of this might be realized in forms, which in particular consist in the development of catalogs and guides, conducting open lectures and workshops, and disseminating information via the mass media and other customarily accepted forms of communication, including social campaigns. Free mediation covers (1) informing the entitled person about the possibilities of using amicable dispute resolution methods, in particular mediation and the benefits resulting from it; (2) preparation of a draft mediation agreement or application for mediation; (3) preparation of a draft application for mediation proceedings in a criminal case; (4) instauration of mediation (5) providing assistance in preparing a court application for approval of a settlement concluded before a mediator. Free mediation does not cover cases in which: (1) a court or other authority has issued a decision to refer the case to mediation or mediation proceedings; (2) there is a reasonable suspicion that there is violence in the parties' relationship.

Free legal aid and free-of-charge civic counseling inure to the benefit of the entitled person who is unable to bear the costs of paid legal assistance, including a natural person running a sole proprietorship who has not employed anyone else during the last year.

Free legal aid is provided in person by a counselor or legal advisor, and in particularly justified circumstances, on their authorization, a legal trainee, or a trainee attorney. Free legal assistance at points entrusted to run a non-governmental organization may also be provided by: (1) a tax advisor – in the field of tax law, with the exception of tax matters related to economic activity; (2) a person who: (a) has graduated in law and holds a master's degree or has completed foreign law studies recognized in the Republic of Poland, (b) has at least three years of experience in performing activities that require legal knowledge and are directly related to the provision of legal aid, (c) enjoys full public rights and has full legal capacity, (d) has not been punished for an intentional offense prosecuted by public prosecution or a tax offense; (3) a mediator in the field of free mediation. Free-of-charge civic counseling may be provided by a person who: (1) has higher education, (2) has completed training in the field of civic counseling with a positive assessment or has experience in providing civic counseling and has obtained a certificate confirming having knowledge and skills in this field, issued by an entity authorized to conduct training and a supplementary course.

A counselor or legal adviser provides free legal aid under an agreement concluded with the district. The district entrusts half of the legal aid points to be run by counselors and legal advisers for the purpose of providing free legal aid, and half to a non-governmental organization conducting public benefit activities for the purpose of providing free legal aid or providing free-of-charge civic counseling.

4. Conclusions

The right to a fair trial, as well as the associated right to a fair hearing and the rights of defence, are fundamental rights of the individual and, concurrently, core values of a democratic state ruled by law; they are derived from this principle and are separately guaranteed by the provisions of international agreements, EU law and national law. The principle of procedural fairness is a system of guarantees allowing the outcome of proceedings to be considered fair, as well as the rights of defence.

The right to free legal aid at the pretrial stage and the right to legal aid in court and administrative court proceedings are integral parts of the above-mentioned rules.

In the literature, plenty of space is devoted to not only the catalog of legal principles, the terminology used in this area, but above all determining their normative or only postulative meaning. In spite of numerous disputes, discussions and polemics, in most cases principles of the law are given a directival character. In this case, it boils down to principles expressed *explicite* in the texts of normative acts or derived from the provisions contained therein using more intricate rules of exegesis. A normative character can also be attributed to the above-mentioned rules, i.e., the principle of the right to a fair trial and the principle of procedural fairness, which in turn is important for the analysis of the problem of free legal aid and the right to legal aid. Hence, these values do not merely represent non-binding postulates, but we include them among fully binding normative rules of operation.

The right to free legal aid at the pretrial stage and the right to legal aid in court and administrative court proceedings are natural standards of a democratic state that facilitate and expand the scope of access to court and allow the outcome of the proceedings to be considered fair, and thus may be recognized as one of the components of the right to a fair trial. Failure to provide free legal aid and the right to legal aid may lead to an infringement of the principle of the right to a fair trial, especially when the individual is in a difficult economic situation and is unable to access professional legal aid from his own resources. The right to free legal aid serves to fulfill its guarantee function at the pretrial stage and implement the legislator's intention to create at this stage a mechanism enabling poor people to obtain legal advice provided by a professional free of charge and to respond to the dysfunctions of the so far scattered and often unprofessional legal advice, which hinders equal access of citizens to justice. Free legal aid is intended to complement the institutions existing in the Polish legal system in court proceedings – legal aid in civil and criminal proceedings and the right to assistance in administrative court proceedings, which allow for exemption from the costs of proceedings or the appointment of a counselor, legal advisor, tax advisor, patent attorney for persons or entities that do not have sufficient funds to cover the costs of a trial or representation.

Taking account of the findings established in this elaboration, one may formulate a thesis according to which the possibility of using free legal aid at the pretrial stage and legal aid (right of assistance) in the process for people in economic disadvantage, are among the core elements of the right to a fair trial, the rights of defence and the principle of procedural fairness. In particular, they effectively extend the scope of the right to a fair trial and serve to ensure equal access to justice. Failure to provide legal aid may constitute an infringement of the abovementioned rules ensuring that citizens have the right to a fair hearing by independent and impartial courts.

Literature

Jabłoński M., *Prawo do nieodpłatnej pomocy prawnej jako „element treści konstytucyjnego prawa do sądu" – uwagi na te postanowień ustawy z 5 sierpnia 2015 r. o nieodpłatnej pomocy prawnej oraz edukacji prawnej*, [in:] A. Hauser, M. Urbaniak (eds.), *Ochrona praw człowieka. Zagadnienia praktyczne*, Poznań 2019.

Kaczocha M., *Ustawa o nieodpłatnej pomocy prawnej i edukacji prawnej*, LEX/el. 2016.

Kmieciak Z., *Idea sprawiedliwości proceduralnej w prawie administracyjnym (Założenia teoretyczne i doświadczenia praktyki)*, „Państwo i Prawo" 1994, z. 10.

Lewandowska K., Lewandowski T., *Organizacja pomocy prawnej*, LEX/e. 2019.

Nowicki M.A., *Europejski Trybunał Praw Człowieka. Wybór orzeczeń 2007*, Warszawa 2008.

Olejniczak-Szałowska E., *Zasada sprawiedliwości proceduralnej*, [in:] M. Stahl (ed.), *Prawo administracyjne. Pojęcia, instytucje, zasady w teorii i orzecznictwie*, Warszawa 2016.

Ploszka A., *Publicznoprawny status jednostki skrajnie ubogiej*, WKP 2019, LEX/el. 2021.

Przywora B., Wróbel A., *Poradnictwo obywatelskie w świetle badań prawnoporównawczych*, Warszawa 2020.

Trociuk S., *Pomoc prawna dla osób ubogich jako forma zapewnienia skutecznego dostępu do krajowego i europejskiego wymiaru sprawiedliwości*, [in:] H. Izdebski, H. Machińska (eds.), *Dostęp obywateli do europejskiego wymiaru sprawiedliwości*, Warszawa 2005.

Zimmermann J., *Prawo administracyjne*, Warszawa 2016.

Hubert Izdebski[1]

Free legal aid – a delegated task of district governments

Abstract: Tasks consisting in providing, and in essence organizing, the provision of free legal aid, thus recognized as public tasks (which also results from art. 47 of the EU CFR), currently represent tasks delegated to the local self-government. This means financing their implementation from the public budget, with the far-reaching possibility of national standardization. This paper represents an attempt to answer the question stated in the title, which requires consideration of the following issues: whether the provision of free out-of-court legal aid should constitute a public task; if that is the case – should it be a government administration task rather than the obligation of a local government? if so – what level of public authorities should be responsible for its implementation in accordance with the subsidiarity principle and taking into account another constitutional principle, i.e. the efficiency of public institutions? Favorable resolution of the first two issues requires consideration of the validity of maintaining the current poviat structure.

Keywords: free legal aid, tasks delegated in the field of government administration, poviat self-government

1. Introduction

Ensuring the provision of free legal aid within the meaning of the Free Legal Aid Act, fundamentally amended on 15 June 2018 as a result of the criticism against the original solutions[2], or – to be more precise – ensuring the provision of pre-trial

1 University SWPS. ORCID: 0000-0002-3390-4167.
2 Journal of Laws item 1467. On the amendment and the legal status after its introduction – B. Przywora, *Normatywny model przedsądowej nieodpłatnej pomocy prawnej w Polsce*, Warsaw 2019, p. 351 et seq. and I. Bentkowska-Furman, *Udział organizacji pozarządowych w zakresie świadczenia usług nieodpłatnej pomocy prawnej, nieodpłatnego poradnictwa obywatelskiego oraz edukacji prawnej*, in: *Organizacje pozarządowe w stuleciu Polski niepodległej*, edited by M. Seroka, Olsztyn 2018, p. 78 et seq. Subsequently, changes in the functioning of the provisions on free legal aid resulted from the state of the COVID-19 epidemic – A. S. Bartnik, K. J. Kowalska,

and out-of-court free legal assistance, is the responsibility of districts *(powiat)* as units of the local government of an intermediate (supra-commune but lower than regional) level in the three-tier local government system in Poland, which was introduced in 1999.

Pursuant to art. 8(1) of the Act:

> "Tasks consisting of providing free legal aid, free civic counselling and legal education [...] shall be delegated tasks within the scope of government administration carried out by a district in consultation with municipalities or independently".

The said provision refers to tasks consisting of providing free legal aid, while at the very beginning of this study, there is the term "ensuring the provision of free legal aid" as the district itself doesn't conduct the activity in question. Its role is essentially limited to organizing the provision of relevant services on the terms as specified in the Act by attorneys-at-law and legal advisers as well as non-governmental organizations appointed in the manner specified in the Act[3]. With respect to running assistance points, there is a statutory rule of an equal division between attorneys-at-law and legal advisers (appointed under a contract concluded annually with the district by the competent professional self-government bodies: the regional bar council and the regional council of the chamber of legal advisers, which sign relevant contacts with the district for this purpose) and non-governmental organizations that conduct a relevant public benefit activity, selected annually in an open tender contest, where at the points run by these organizations, the assistance may also be provided, apart from the attorneys-at-law and legal advisers with whom the organization has signed a contract, by tax advisers in the field of tax law (excluding that relating to business activity) and masters of law with at least three-year experience in performing activities that require legal knowledge directly related to the provision of legal aid.

The district's tasks being discussed are statutorily defined as delegated tasks within the scope of government administration. Such a definition is not present in the fundamental statute governing districts' structure, namely the Act of 5 June 1998 on District Self-Government[4] – which refers to "matters falling within the scope of districts' operations as tasks within the scope of government administration performed by the districts". However, it is anchored in art. 166(2) of the Constitution RP, forming the second constitutional category of tasks of local government units apart from their own tasks of first importance[5]. The definition is also

---

A. Krzysztofowicz, *Nieodpłatna pomoc prawna online w czasach epidemii,* LEX/el 2020.

3 This is pointed out, in particular, by D. E. Lach, *Nieodpłatna pomoc prawna jako instrument zabezpieczenia społecznego,* "Ruch Prawniczy, Ekonomiczny i Socjologiczny" 2016, Vol. 3, p. 21 et seq.

4 Journal of Laws of 2020, item 920.

5 *"If it arises from the state's justified needs, a statute may delegate the performance of other public tasks to local government units. The statute shall specify the transferring*

present in the Act of 8 March 1990 on Municipal Self-Government[6] and, above all, in statutes on financing delegate tasks: the Act of 13 November 2003 on Income of Local Government Units[7] and the Act of 27 August 2009 on Public Finances[8]; thus, its content is also straightforward with respect to districts.

The content comes down to the fact that the performance of delegated tasks is to be financed from the central budget by means of designated subsidies, the amount of which, pursuant to art. 49(1) and (5) of the Act on Income of Local Government Units, should enable the performance of these tasks and, at the same time, should be transferred in a manner making the complete and timely performance of the delegated tasks possible; it can be added that the practice doesn't always reflect the statutory obligations[9]. Chapter 5 of the Free Legal Aid Act specifies the method for determining and allocating subsidies granted to districts as part of the state budget at the disposal of voivodes, who are representatives of the Council of Ministers in the voivodeship according to art. 152(1) of the Constitution RP.

The said provision of the Free Legal Aid Act demonstrates one more important feature of free legal aid that is to be provided by the district government on the terms as specified in this Act. The district may carry out the tasks in this field on its own, which is a rule as regards delegated tasks, but it may also perform them in consultation with municipalities. It means that although the task has not been delegated to municipalities, which are closest to residents, these basic local government units can be involved, on a voluntary basis, in the provision of free legal aid – which is part of a wider yet still not fully systematically treated area of public and social activities aimed at providing citizens with access to knowledge about their rights and access to the administration of justice, and, simultaneously, aimed at exercising the right to social security and at supporting families[10].

This study is an attempt to answer the question of whether the legislator chose a good solution when assigning the task of providing free legal aid to the districts

---

procedure and the manner of performing their own tasks. Cf. H. Izdebski, *Komentarz do Konstytucji RP. Art. 15, 16, 163–172,* Warsaw 2020, p. 225 at seq., p. 230 at seq.

6 Journal of Laws of 2020, item 71, as amended. On the other hand, in the Act of 5 June 1998 on Voivodeship Self-Government (Journal of Laws of 2020, item 1668), the wording corresponding to that adopted in the Act on District Self-Government is used.

7 Journal of Laws of 2020, item 23, as amended.

8 Journal of Laws of 2021, item 305.

9 Cf., for example, H. Izdebski, *Samorząd terytorialny. Pionowy podział władzy,* Warsaw 2020, p. 154 at seq.

10 An attempt at a broader approach to the issue of free legal aid going beyond the Act of 5 December 2015, also in sociological terms, was made in: A. S. Bartnik, K. J. Kowalska, *Nieodpłatna pomoc prawna,* Warsaw 2019. On social aspects of free legal aid – A. Szluz, *Nieodpłatna przedsądowa pomoc prawna jako forma wsparcia rodziny,* [in:] B. Szluz, A. Szluz, M. Urbańska (eds.), *Współczesna rodzina. Aspekty społeczno-prawne,* Rzeszów 2017 and B. Przywora, *Normatywny model...,* p. 205 at seq.

as a delegated task within the scope of government administration. To answer this question, three issues have to be considered in turn:

- should the provision of free out-of-court legal aid in a broader sense constitute a public task?
- if so, should it be a task within the scope of government administration?
- and finally, if an answer to the second of the above questions is affirmative, the following issue may be raised: which level of public authorities should be assigned with carrying out this task in compliance with the principle of subsidiarity and considering the principle of efficient operation of public institutions also referred to in the preamble of the Constitution RP?

2. Should the provision of free out-of-court legal aid in a broader sense constitute a public task?

As for the first question, it is hard not to assume – and this is indirectly done in art. 2(2) of the Free Legal Aid Act[11] – that the provision of free legal aid can be the subject of activities of entities that are not public authorities, in particular, apart from activities of not only self-governments of attorneys-at-law and legal advisers (which, however, are specific bodies of decentralized public authority) but also individuals performing, in this case pro bono, these professions of public trust, activities of non-governmental organizations within the framework of their statutory operations.

The role of non-governmental organizations was emphasized, also to enable them to provide legal assistance under the Act in question, by the introduction of art. 4(1) of the Act of 24 April 2003 on Public Benefit and Volunteer Work[12], which defines the sphere of public benefit work with respect of the point: *"providing free legal aid and increasing public awareness"*. The Act on Public Benefit Work simultaneously provides a formal and legal argument in favor of the affirmative answer to the first question. The fact that the provision of free legal aid, which, as it can be seen, has been directly included in the sphere of public benefit work, constitutes the fulfillment of public tasks follows directly from the definition of public benefit work provided in art. 3(1) of the Act: *"socially beneficial work performed by non-governmental organizations in the sphere of public tasks specified in the Act"*.

Apart from the formal and legal argument, the affirmative answer is also, and above all, supported by a premise of a substantive nature. Organizing a properly operating system of free legal aid should be considered a public task on the ground that it serves as an essential though obviously not the only, as already indicated, a legal instrument for ensuring the execution of at least two fundamental rights: the

---

11 *"This Act shall not limit activities in the field of free legal counselling, civic counselling and legal education"*.

12 Journal of Laws of 2020, item 1057.

right to an effective legal remedy and a fair trial and the right to social security in a broad sense. This is directly reflected in the second and third sentence of art. 47(2) of the CFR:

> Everyone shall have the possibility of being advised, defended, and represented. Legal aid shall be made available to those who lack sufficient resources in so far as such aid is necessary to ensure effective access to justice.

In the explanatory statement of the government's bill of 2015[13], it was stated that this was to create a system of assistance for citizens within the framework of the administration of justice in a broad sense and, at the same time, one of the instruments of the state's social policy implemented by state institutions or non-governmental organizations.

Therefore, the answer to the first question has to be unambiguously affirmative. Providing free legal aid to citizens in need has all the characteristics of a public task. In a state under the rule of law, which, it must be born in mind, cannot function without the fiction of common knowledge of law, this is, moreover, a very important public task.

3. Should the provision of free out-of-court legal aid in a broader sense be a task within the scope of government administration?

An answer to the second question may seem similarly affirmative for the same reasons, all the more so that the principle of equality before the law and, thus, equal treatment cannot be ignored. In the justification for the bill, it was indicated in any case that it was a task within the scope of government administration as there was a need for standards for providing aid made uniform at the state level and effective supervision over the compliance with those standards, as well as a permanent source of financing. It was also indicated that the then proposed and consequently adopted Act was aimed at creating a system initiated by the Act of 28 November 2014 on Protection of and Assistance to Victims and Witnesses[14], which had transposed two EU directives. The authority performing the tasks specified in the latter Act is the provincial police commander and, thus, unquestionably, a government administration body. Another thing is that these tasks are far from the provision of free legal aid, and, therefore, the system that was to be developed (and has not altogether been created yet) was understood very broadly.

It can be taken for granted that there are no structures within the government administration that could perform the tasks being discussed. Creating separate government agencies would also hardly be considered advisable considering the

13 Print no. 338 of the 7th-term Sejm of the Republic of Poland.
14 Journal of Laws of 2015, item 21.

option of using the institution of delegating tasks to local government units, which is also supported by the principle of subsidiarity in its classic vertical representation. It must also be kept in mind that in the light of judicial decisions of the Constitutional Tribunal from the period of its regular operation, the difference between local government units' own and delegated tasks is that in respect of the latter, the role of local government authorities consists in executive functions rather than creative ones, because the Act defines the manner of their execution, while in respect of the former, local government authorities must have appropriate freedom if not in creating, then at least in deciding on the methods of performing the tasks[15]. As already mentioned, the explanatory statement of the bill of 2015 stated the need to apply standards for providing aid made uniform at the state level, which excludes the discretion of local governments, and one of the guarantees of the uniformity of actions is to ensure a permanent source of their financing pursuant to the algorithms specified in the Act. These are undoubtedly arguments in favor of the governmental nature of the task.

This could have concluded the answer to the second question, but for the fact that there are statutorily defined tasks in the field of legal counseling, which are parallel to no small extent, classified as the local government's own tasks rather than delegated tasks within the scope of government administration.

These are, in particular:

- legal specialist counseling (art. 36(2)(g) and art. 46(1) and (2) of the Act of 12 March 2004 on Social Assistance[16]) provided to people and families who encounter difficulties or demonstrate a need for support in solving their life problems, regardless of their income, performed by providing information on applicable provisions in the field of family and guardianship law, social security, protection of tenants' rights;
- free consumer counseling and legal information on the protection of consumer interests (art. 42(1)(1) in connection with art. 39 of the Act of 16 February 2007 on Competition and Consumer Protection)[17].

These are tasks assigned to a district, performed with the help of its special agencies – a district family support center (but also attorneys-at-law, legal advisers, and non-governmental organizations) and a consumer ombudsman, respectively.

Even when acknowledging that especially the matter of social assistance, which includes legal specialist counseling, is of a nature that requires acting in close connection with local needs, it is difficult not to notice the lack of consistency in qualifying materially overlapping tasks, which results from the absence, maintained despite the adoption of the Free Legal Aid Act and its amendment of

---

15 Cf., in particular, judgment of the CT of 25 July 2006, K 30/04, OTK-A 2006 No. 7, item 86.

16 Journal of Laws of 2020, item 1876, as amended.

17 Journal of Laws of 2021, item 275.

15 June 2018, of a substantively systemic approach to the matter of free legal assistance not related to free legal aid provided "ex officio" in the course of proceedings before courts, regulated in individual procedural laws. If it is acknowledged that free legal aid should have uniform standards and stable sources of algorithmically determined financing, it may be necessary to recognize its various institutions as the performance of tasks within the scope of government administration and even state tasks, if relevant powers of courts are considered.

5. Which level of public authorities should be assigned with carrying out this task in compliance with the principle of subsidiarity and considering the principle of efficient operation of public institutions also referred to in the preamble of the Constitution RP?

Following the comments made so far, an answer to the last of the three questions posed arrives at two levels.

The first level is a minimalist, and perhaps also realistic when considering how it should be, start with the status, in which the district is assigned with the task of providing free legal aid not only under the Free Legal Aid Act, but also other indicated statutes. With this approach, one should talk about the maximum statutory unification, and certainly coordination, of the performance of these tasks as tasks delegated to the district.

The second level involves – assuming that it is impossible to justify the creation of relevant government agencies and that decentralization rather than further recentralization is needed – breaking away from the current situation, and this in twofold direction:

- firstly, as regards a possible new division of tasks (delegated ones, as already mentioned) among the current levels of local government units, corresponding to the constitutional principles of subsidiarity and, at the same time, efficiency of operation of public institutions;
- secondly, in respect of the district's current structure itself and, thus, a place for the tasks in question in a possibly different structure of the local government, which would be a maximalist approach.

In the first case, it seems necessary to assume that little can be done but accept that one is dealing with tasks of a level higher than the municipality. More than a quarter of Polish municipalities counts up to 5,000 residents, and a half of them – less than 7,500 residents[18]. On the other hand, the voivodships may be too large, especially since the initial idea of tasks of the voivodeship government (admittedly

18 Central Statistical Office, *Powierzchnia i ludność w przekroju terytorialnym w 2020 r.*, table 12.

its own tasks) was that that government was not to provide services of an administrative nature to individual citizens. Nevertheless, the fact remains that districts were assigned with tasks – in general and in the scope being discussed – quite accidentally and arbitrarily, without considering other subjective variants of their fulfillment[19]. However, it would be difficult to ponder such considerations on the assumption that the current self-government structure is maintained – unless it is recognized that the tasks of providing free legal aid may, and perhaps should, be carried out outside the territorial self-government by, for example, self-governments of attorneys-at-law and legal advisers[20].

6. Conclusions

This allows for a – maximalist – return to the discussion, recurring from time to time, about the very traditional shape given to districts in 1998 and even about searching for an appropriate number of their tasks then and later. In the Free Legal Aid Act, it is assumed that there should be at least two aid points in a district, and the basis for calculating the multiplier per point is 25,000 residents. In the meantime, 16 % of "land" districts count less than 50,000 inhabitants, including 5 districts with less than 30,000; therefore, either they don't match the law, or the law doesn't match them. It is worth adding that more than half of the "land" districts have less than 75,000 residents – while it seems to follow from the Act that optimal solutions for a district start with three legal aid points. Regardless of the indicated statutory standards, some districts are simply too small to properly organize a network of legal aid with their "own" insufficient human resources, including lawyers and legal advisers residing in their area.

Units of NUTS level 3 would be much more efficient in this regard – except that they have not been administrative units in our country since 1998. Larger districts would also be more efficient than the present ones. The fact that districts are too small has drawn attention since 1998. However, no initiatives have been introduced to change this state of affairs, which also becomes more permanent, because districts not only refer, as a rule, to tradition (another thing is that this tradition doesn't date back earlier than to the nineteenth century), but they have not only reached the age of majority but also the time limit of a new generation. The search for a systemically structured and, consequently, efficient organization of free legal aid, along with certain other matters assigned to local governments though included within the scope of government administration (in particular, it

---

19 K. Bandarzewski, *Udzielanie nieodpłatnej pomocy prawnej jako zadanie zlecone powiatów,* [in:] M. Stec, S. Płażek (eds.), *Charakter i konstrukcja zadań samorządu terytorialnego,* Warsaw 2017, p. 17 et seq. Similarly: W. Baranowska-Zając, *Prawna ochrona konsumenta jako zadanie samorządu terytorialnego – potrzeba reinterpretacji?,* in: ibid., p. 36 et seq.

20 Cf. K. Bandarzewski, *Udzielanie nieodpłatnej pomocy...*

may apply to construction supervision), could become a premise for sparking off a – necessary – debate about the territorial division of the state more adjusted to the needs of the third decade of the twenty-first century.

Literature

Bandarzewski K., *Udzielanie nieodpłatnej pomocy prawnej jako zadanie zlecone powiatów,* [in:] M. Stec, S. Płażek (eds.), *Charakter i konstrukcja zadań samorządu terytorialnego,* Warszawa 2017.

Baranowska-Zając W., *Prawna ochrona konsumenta jako zadanie samorządu terytorialnego – potrzeba reinterpretacji?,* [in:] M. Stec, S. Płażek (eds.), *Charakter i konstrukcja zadań samorządu terytorialnego,* Warszawa 2017.

Bartnik A. S., Kowalska K. J., Krzysztofowicz A., *Nieodpłatna pomoc prawna on line w czasach epidemii,* LEX/el 2020.

Bentkowska-Furman I., *Udział organizacji pozarządowych w zakresie świadczenia usług nieodpłatnej pomocy prawnej, nieodpłatnego poradnictwa obywatelskiego oraz edukacji prawnej,* [in:] M. Seroka (ed.), *Organizacje pozarządowe w stuleciu Polski niepodległej,* Olsztyn 2018.

Izdebski H., *Komentarz do Konstytucji RP. Art. 15, 16, 163–172,* Warszawa 2020.

Izdebski H., *Samorząd terytorialny. Pionowy podział władzy,* Warszawa 2020.

Lach D. E., *Nieodpłatna pomoc prawna jako instrument zabezpieczenia społecznego,* „Ruch Prawniczy, Ekonomiczny i Socjologiczny" 2016 z. 3.

Przywora B., *Normatywny model przedsądowej nieodpłatnej pomocy prawnej w Polsce,* Warszawa 2019.

Szluz A., *Nieodpłatna przedsądowa pomoc prawna jako forma wsparcia rodziny,* [in:] B. Szluz, A. Szluz, M. Urbańska (eds.), *Współczesna rodzina. Aspekty społeczno-prawne,* Rzeszów 2017.

Bartosz Majchrzak[1]

The scope of the concept of "civic counseling" in the Act on free legal aid, free civic counseling and legal education

Abstract: The preliminary research assumption was that the introduction of the civic counseling structure to the Act on Free Legal Aid, Free Civic Counseling and Legal Education (UNPP) "overlapped" the hitherto semantic chaos associated with this concept and the multitude of affined terms relating to legal support for the poor and the lack of a uniform normative understanding. In this context, we set the objective of the paper, i.e., the answer to the question: Do the provisions of the UNPP define "civic counseling" in a clear and precise manner, or whether establishing the meaning of this notion is still hampered and requires advanced interpretative procedures. Thus, the scope of analysis was restricted to the narrow issue of the normative meaning of this concept in the specified fragment of the regulation. In the fact of that, the followed detailed hypotheses were accepted: (1) the concept of "civic counseling", presented in either a "non-adjective" form or bearing the adjective "free", must be interpreted uniformly throughout the Act and reduced to the meaning stemming from art. 3a UNPP; (2) civic counseling is an activity that meets all the conditions listed in art. 3a UNPP; (3) the meaning of "civic counseling" should be clarified from the negative side, by distinguishing it from providing legal aid, providing legal consultations and legal information.

Keywords: civic counseling, free legal aid, legal aid

1. Introduction

The legal architecture (including the legal definition) of civic counseling was introduced to the Free Legal Aid Act, under the Act of 15 June 2018 amending the act on free legal aid and legal education and certain other acts[2]. It is interesting to note that the amendment in the above-mentioned scope was supposed to constitute a specific complement to the "system of assistance to citizens within the broadly

1 Cardinal Stefan Wyszyński Univeristy in Warsaw. ORCID: 0000-0001-5336-6717.
2 Journal of Laws item 1467; further: the amending act.

understood administration of justice" functioning at the pretrial stage[3]. Concurrently, as described in the justification of the draft amending act, civic counseling is a "proven and valued form of assistance in Poland and other countries"[4]. Expressed another way, its regulation in the UNPP provisions was, as it were, "imposed" on the practice of this type of counseling, pursued in particular by the network of civic counseling offices associated in the Union of Citizens' Advice Bureaus, as well as by other organizations[5]. This circumstance resulted in, among others, the fact that the statutory definition of the discussed legal structure in art. 3a UNPP encountered "existing" definitions, and especially the hitherto semantic chaos related to the notion of "civic counseling"[6], a multitude of "synonymous" terms relating to legal support for the poor (i.e., legal aid, legal counseling, counseling (non-adjective), legal aid, the poor law, providing legal information) and the lack of a common understanding[7].

Against the above results of "preliminary research", the fundamental goal of this study is to reflect on whether the provisions of the UNPP define the concept of "civic counseling" in a clear and precise manner, or whether establishing the meaning of this notion is still hampered and requires advanced interpretative procedures. Thus, the scope of the analysis was limited to the narrow issue of the normative meaning of the mentioned concept based on the indicated fragment of the legal regulation, namely the Act on Legal Aid, Free-of-charge Civic Counseling and Legal Education.

For a research objective shaped in this way, we assumed the following detailed hypotheses: (1) the term "civic counseling", presented in either "non-adjective" form or provided with the adjective "free-of-charge", should be understood – as

3 See justification of the draft act on free legal aid, free legal information and legal education of the society, appendix no. 3338/term VII, p. 1; see also A. S. Bartnik, K. J. Kowalska, *Poradnictwo prawne i obywatelskie w kontekście świadomości prawnej i potrzeby edukacji prawnej Polaków. Wybrane problemy*, „Studia Iuridica" 2018, no. LXXVIII, p. 49; B. Przywora, A. Wróbel, *Poradnictwo obywatelskie w świetle badań prawnoporównawczych*, Warszawa 2020, p. 10, https://iws.gov.pl/wp-content/uploads/2021/01/IWS_Przywora-B.-Wr%C3%B3bel-A._Poradnictwo-obywatelskie-w-%C5%9Bwietle-bada%C5%84-prawnopor%C3%B3wnawczych.pdf; (accessed: 3.12.2023).

4 Justification of the draft act amending the act on free legal aid and legal education and certain other acts, appendix no. 1868/term VIII, p. 3.

5 A. S. Bartnik, K. J. Kowalska, op. cit., p. 55; M. Parlicki, *Poradnictwo obywatelskie jako aktywizacyjna forma pomocy oferowana jednostkom i rodzinom*, „Państwo i Społeczeństwo" 2012, no. 4, pp. 123–126.

6 See I. Henning, *O poradnictwie prawnym i obywatelskim*, [in:] I. Henning, A. Rozkosz (eds.), *Poradnik dla doradczyń i doradców poradnictwa prawnego i obywatelskiego*, Warszawa 2014, pp. 18–22; M. Parlicki, op. cit., pp. 115–120.

7 See T. Schimanek, G. Wiaderek, *Poradnictwo prawne i obywatelskie – pojęcie, jakość, efektywność*, [in:] *Czym jest poradnictwo prawne i obywatelskie*, Warszawa 2011, pp. 3–4.

regards the features, types and subject of activities – uniformly throughout the Act and reduced to the meaning resulting from art. 3a UNPP; (2) civic counseling is an activity that meets jointly the conditions set out in art. 3a(1) the first sentence and (2) of the UNPP, differentiated in terms of subject matter – concerning at least all of the areas specified in art. 3a(1) the second sentence, UNPP; (3) clarification of the term "providing civic counseling" should also take place from the negative side, by distinguishing it from providing legal assistance within the meaning of 3 UNPP, providing legal advice and information, and providing legal education; (4) introduction of art. 3a of the UNPP was normatively justified due to the specific legal obligations provided for in the provisions of the UNPP.

The conducted analysis justifies the formulation of the thesis that the decoding of the normative meaning of the concept of civic counseling in the UNPP requires its reconstruction not only based on art. 3a of the UNPP, but also in the context of a number of other provisions of this Act (which in this case stresses the special role of the systemic and purposeful interpretation of the relevant regulations). Supporting this thesis, as well as achieving the determined objective of the elaboration, including verification of the assumed research hypotheses inherently required the use of the dogmatic method, understood in a "classic" way – following E. Jarra – as a legal study which, taking a positive, binding law as an attitude, lays it out systematically, i.e. in the order of a logical grouping of legal material; it removes possible gaps and contradictions, explaining the considerable meaning of the provisions, producing definitions of legal concepts and going further to developing principles-guidelines that permeate the legislation[8].

2. "Civic counseling" and "free-of-charge civic counseling"

It must be stated first that under the provisions of the UNPP, the term "civic counseling" occurs primarily with the adjective "free of charge" and in this formula it was defined normatively in art. 3a of the UNPP. Nonetheless, the listed term is used in the act independently as well, i.e., without being specified with the word "free-of-charge" (see art. 2, art. 4a (7), art. 11(3a) point 2, art. 11a sections 1–2, art. 11b sections 2 and 5, art. 11d (2) point 1, (3) point 1 and (8) point 1 of the UNPP). Against this background, it is worth reflecting on whether in both these contexts we are dealing with the same referent of the analyzed name, only sometimes nuanced by the "free" characteristic, or whether it is about significantly different terms of reference.

The pursuit of meaning of the term "civic counseling" (including "the provision of civic counseling" appearing in particular in art. 4a (7) or art. 11b (2) of the UNPP) should consider as priority what role in the legal interpretation is assigned to legal definitions. Legal definitions are designed to guarantee the most important

8 E. Jarra, *Ogólna teorja prawa*, Warszawa 1922, p. 17.

postulated features in the text of a normative act, i.e., its adequacy to the intention of the legislator (a legal provision serves to express the intentions of the legislator as precisely and faithfully as possible)[9]. From here, a consequence can be made in the form of an order to "search" for this type of definition in the legal text. In this case it translates into the need to ascribe a meaning to the concept of civic counseling, which results from the term "free-of-charge civic counseling" specified more precisely in art. 3a of the UNPP, which is slightly different from the definition analyzed under this study. Since the legislator's "intention" is to clarify an element of the subject of protection in such a way, then all detailed regulations containing the same conceptual core must be interpreted in the spirit of specifying this subject and are somewhat subordinated to it. Also, the statement regarding the harmonized understanding of "civic counseling" on the statutory basis is justified in the wake of one of the fundamental guidelines of linguistic interpretation, i.e., the terminological consistency directive, according to which the same legal language phrases should not be given different meanings[10]. Therefore, the term "civic counseling" used in art. 2, art. 4a para. 7, art. 11 sec. 3a, point 2, art. 11a para. 1–2, art. 11b para. 2 and 5, art. 11d para. 2 point 1, sec. 3 point 1 and sec. 8 point 1 of the UNPP is the same term as in art. 3a of the UNPP, yet one which was clarified by adding a specifying feature (i.e., marked with the adjective "free-of-charge").

Furthermore, it is worth noting that the *definiens* included in art. 3a of the UNPP, in fact, comes down exclusively to determining the characteristics, types and objects of a specified activity ("activities tailored to the individual situation of the entitled person, aimed at raising the awareness of that person about his/her rights or obligations and support in solving the problem independently, including if necessary, drawing up an action plan together with an authorized person and assisting in its implementation. [...] In particular advice for indebted persons and advice on housing and social security matters. [...] also includes free mediation"), however, it does not specify the occurrence in *definiendum* of the term "free", leaving them somewhat outside the scope of concern (moreover – beyond "free mediation" – *definiens* does not refer to it at all). This reveals the legislator's desire to establish a uniform – for the purposes of the entire act – understanding of the concept of civic counseling, presented in the provisions of the UNPP in the form of either "adjectival" (e.g., art. 2 UNPP) or bearing the adjective "free-of-charge" (e.g., art. 1 of the UNPP). The semantic difference between them is that the former activity – due to the lack of an appropriate restriction – can be both paid and free of charge, while the other is based on unpaid benefits. In other words, "civic counseling" and "free-of-charge civic counseling" are undoubtedly generically the same activity, which is defined in art. 3a of the UNPP.

9 Cf. T. Chauvin, T. Stawecki, P. Winczorek, *Wstęp do prawoznawstwa*, Warszawa 2016, p. 82.

10 L. Morawski, *Zasady wykładni prawa*, Toruń 2006, pp. 104–105.

The result of the interpretation brought forward also strengthens the reference to the purposeful aspect of the analyzed provisions. Since the entities listed in art. 4a para. 7, art. 11 sec. 3a, art. 11b para. 2 and 5 and art. 11d para. 3 and 8 of the UNPP serve to provide free-of-charge civic counseling or conduct training and supplementary courses preparing for this type of activity, the rationality requirements dictate that these entities are adequately experienced with respect to the activity that is to be the subject of it. This would in turn point that the so-called adjectiveless "civic counseling" must be identical in content and subject matter to "free-of-charge civic counseling" as defined in art. 3a of the UNPP. The purpose of the above-mentioned provisions is to provide the highest quality services in the field of free-of-charge civic counseling, including an appropriate level of training or courses preparing for this activity (see also art. 11a (1–2) of the UNPP), provided by an entity with experience, knowledge and skills with respect to this area.

3. Legal definition of "civic counseling" and its interpretative contexts

As stated by the Provincial Administrative Court in Warsaw in its judgment of 26 September 2019, II SA/Wa 850/19, art. 3a of the UNPP contains a "very vague definition of the concept considered". Additionally, the court pointed out that the use of the phrase "in particular" by the legislator testifies to the open and merely exemplary nature of this definition. Such a vague definition of the concept of "civic counseling" implies an obligation to interpret the above phrase.

With regard to the normative content of the analyzed term, resulting from art. 3a of the UNPP, it should be noted that it relates to an activity, that has the following cumulative characteristics: (1) it is adjusted to the individual circumstances of the entitled person; (2) it aims to raise the awareness of this person about his/her rights or obligations; (3) it provides support in independent problem-solving by that person; (4) it includes – if necessary – preparation of an action plan together with an authorized person and assistance in the implementation of that plan as well as mediation in terms of art. 4a of the UNPP; (5) it is subject to differentiation, as in total it includes at least advice for indebted persons, advice on housing and social security matters. Simultaneously we should reemphasize the need for the occurrence of all the above characteristics simultaneously to be able to call it civic counseling within the meaning of the analyzed normative act. This clearly indicates the normative context of the use of this term in individual provisions of the UNPP (see in particular art. 11a (1) the first sentence, and (2) the second sentence of the UNPP). The exception to this rule (confirming, in essence, the correctness of the formulated conclusion) stems from those statutory regulations which constitute the specialization of on-call duty, during which free-of-charge civic counseling is provided (e.g., art. 8 (9), art. 8a (1) (2), art. 9 (1) (1) (d) of the UNPP). This would then be limited to a designated area of law or issues, or addressed in particular to a concrete group of entitled persons or will only cover free mediation (see art. 8 (9) and (13) of the UNPP).

In the framework of art. 3a of the UNPP, it is worth noting that, in particular, the condition of raising the awareness of the entitled person about their rights or obligations may *prima facie* interfere with the delineation of providing civic counseling from (free) legal aid (cf. art. 3(1) (1) UNPP), providing legal advice or legal information (e.g., art. 11d (2) (1) and (3) (1) UNPP) or conducting legal education (cf. art. 3b (1) (1) of the UNPP). Nonetheless, the semantic differences of these concepts are evident, provided that the above rule of cumulative occurrence of the features of civic counseling is considered and supplemented by defining this term from the negative side as well through its confrontation with the understanding of other concepts perceived by the legislator as "synonymous" (similar in spectrum) provisions of the UNPP (due to their subordination to the same goal of legal regulation). These include specifically "(free) legal aid" and "providing legal advice, legal information"; these terms often appear in the immediate vicinity of the concept of civic counseling, and what is more – they are often separated from it by the inseparable conjunction "or" (see e.g., art. 4a (7) and (8), art. 7 (1), art. 11d (2) (1) and (3) (1) of the UNPP), which may signal the legislator's lower emphasis on semantic distinctions. That said, this does not imply the possibility of withdrawing from the rule of prohibiting a synonymous interpretation (according to which different phrases of the legal language should not be given the same meaning[11]). It is worth supplementing the above calculation with "legal education", which is clearly distinguished in relation to civic counseling (cf. e.g., art. 2, art. 7a (1) or art. 11 (7) UNPP), especially by using the conjunction "and", i.e., having an enumerational meaning[12].

Consequently, the term "civic counseling" should also be construed with the use of "negative definition". In other words, despite certain similarities to "free legal aid", the analyzed concept represents an activity other than that which consists (only) in: (1) informing a natural person about the applicable legal status and his/her rights or obligations, including in connection with pending preparatory, administrative, court or administrative court proceedings; (2) indicating to the entitled person the method of solving his legal problem; (3) drawing up a draft letter in the matters referred to in points 1 and 2, with the exception of pleadings in pending preparatory or court proceedings and letters in pending administrative court proceedings, (4) drawing up a draft letter for exemption from paying court fees or appointing an ex officio attorney in court proceedings or appointing a counselor, legal advisor, tax advisor or patent attorney in administrative court proceedings and informing about the costs of the proceedings and the financial risk related to bringing the case to court (art. 3 para. 1 of the UNPP). Citizen counseling also does not constitute (only) "providing legal advice" (i.e., developing

11 L. Morawski, op. cit., p 103.
12 Cf. Z. Ziembiński, *Logika praktyczna*, Warszawa 1997, p. 86.

and providing reliable, specific and individualized sets of information relating to the presented legal problem and, if necessary, assistance in solving it until the case enters the judicial phase of the proceedings[13]) nor is it limited to providing "legal information" (i.e., providing information on legal regulations relating to the situation of the reporting entity). These "negative" semantic aspects of the analyzed concept were also stressed in the justification to the draft amending act. In the light of this act, civic counseling "will facilitate [...], for those who have received counseling and who may experience some difficulties in understanding the complex legal language, using in full the acquired knowledge in practice [...]." Civic counseling undoubtedly facilitates navigation in the legal system, prevents social marginalization of people who use counseling, helps solve the problems of people who are already excluded, and thus paves the way for their reentry into society[14]. It should be reminded here that in the case of justification of the draft, we are dealing with the so-called authentic interpretation, revealing the real intentions of the legislator, which guided him in the effort to create legal provisions appropriate to the implementation of these intentions. This represents a substantial argument in favor of accepting this interpretative result of the analyzed concept as binding.

Separating civic counseling from "legal education" should not, in turn, pose serious difficulties, as the latter institution – although it also aims to impart knowledge about civic rights and obligations – is nevertheless addressed to the general public (see art. 3b of the UNPP) and not to an individualized addressee (like in the case of civic counseling or legal assistance).

Assistance in resolving "borderline" situations, including those incorporating an element of the "common set" of legal definitions of civil counseling and free legal assistance, i.e., free mediation (see art. 3 (1) (3a) and art. 3a (2) UNPP), consists in referring to the criterion of an entity undertaking a certain activity. Legal assistance is provided by a counselor, legal advisor, and in particularly justified cases, an advocate trainee or a trainee solicitor (art. 5 (1) UNPP) and – in the points entrusted to running a non-governmental organization – a tax advisor (in the field of tax law) or a person who has graduated from law school, obtained a master's degree or completed foreign law studies recognized in the Republic of Poland and has at least three years of experience in performing activities requiring legal knowledge directly related to the provision of legal aid (art. 11 (1) and (2) of the UNPP). On the other hand, the provision of civic counseling requires having higher education and successfully completing training in this field or having relevant experience and obtaining an appropriate certificate confirming knowledge and skills in this area (art. 11 (3a) of the UNPP).

Elements of the negative definition of civic counseling are complemented by the reference to the feature specified in art. 3a sec. 1 the second sentence, UNPP.

---

13 B.a., *System nieodpłatnego poradnictwa prawnego i obywatelskiego w Polsce*, Warszawa 2013, p. 8.

14 *Uzasadnienie projektu ustawy o zmianie ustawy ...*, p. 3.

It boils down to listing the three key areas of civic counseling that must be jointly practiced by an entity in order for it to meet the minimum *sine qua non* condition so that its activity can be considered as civic counseling within the meaning of the Act. Previously, this premise was defined as an appropriate subject differentiation of this counseling. In other words, civic counseling in view of art. 3a UNPP will not be providing counseling with a narrow scope, in particular not covering all three of the above categories, and limited, for example, only to providing advice to indebted persons or only to advice on counteracting domestic violence. Support for this statement can be additionally found in the relevant provisions of the UNPP, especially in art. 8a sec. 1 of this act. Against this background, reference should be made to the rules of linguistic interpretation and the resulting directives of the varying understandings of phrases that have a different sound. This provision differentiates civic counseling and counseling in specific, individual areas (i.e. family counseling, psychological, pedagogical, social welfare counseling, on solving alcohol problems and other addictions, on counteracting domestic violence, as part of crisis intervention, for the unemployed, for victims of crime, in the field of consumer rights, children's rights, patient's rights, social security, labor law, tax law, for people in a dispute with financial market entities). This determines the conclusion about the comprehensive nature of the activity specified in art. 3a of the UNPP, covering at least the provision of advice to indebted persons in the field of housing and social security.

4. Basic implications of the adopted definition of "civic counseling"

As already explained, on the basis of the regulations of the UNPP, the concept of civic counseling often appears in the immediate vicinity of the term "legal aid", representing a separate conjunction of an inseparable alternative "or", which may suggest that there is no need for a precise distinction between these two types of activities. But that would be an invalid conclusion. Demarcating an explicit semantic border for "civic counselling" is necessary from the point of view of: (1) evaluation of whether the performance of the public task (art. 8 (1) UNPP) has been implemented correctly in terms of complying with the requirement of 11 sec. 1b and 1c UNPP; (2) establishing the competence of the persons mentioned in art. 11 sec. 3a UNPP; (3) identification of the subject of training and supplementary courses referred to in Art. 11a para. 1 and 2 UNPP; (4) indication of the entity authorized to conduct such training and courses identified in art. 11b para. 2 UNPP. It is worth remarking that in practice, particularly the latter context of the existence of the concept of civic counseling raises some doubts over their interpretation. Hence, it is only justified to devote some more space to it.

The implemented arrangements which refer to the interpretation of the term "civic counseling" mean that the right to conduct training and supplementary courses for counselors may only be granted to an entity associating non-governmental organizations that provided – for a fee or free of charge – civic counseling within the meaning of art. 3a of the UNPP (art. 11b (2) UNPP) during the specified period. Hence, these conditions are not met by non-governmental organizations with experience in the form of providing only legal assistance, providing legal advice or legal information within the meaning of art. 3 UNPP, art. 4 sec. 1 point 1b of the Act of 24 April 2003 on Public Benefit and Volunteer Work, or in the plain (natural) sense of these terms. This semantic intuition is expressly confirmed by the legislator by referring to art. 11b para. 2 UNPP only to units providing civic counseling, while other provisions of this Act are addressed to entities performing at least one of the above-mentioned types of activity, i.e., legal aid, civic counseling, providing legal advice or legal information (see e.g., art. 11 para. 7 and 10 and art. 11d (2) (1) of the UNPP). Therefore, if the intention of the legislator expressed in art. 11b para. 2 of the UNPP was to grant powers to those non-governmental organizations which dealt only with providing legal assistance, legal advice or legal information until the application was submitted to the Minister of Justice (see art. 11b (3) UNPP), it would be *expressis verbis* articulated (similarly as it was done, for example, in art. 11d (2) (1) of the UNPP).

In consequence of the adoption of the requirement of the entity's comprehensiveness referred to in art. 3a UNPP (including at least providing advice to indebted persons in the field of housing and social security), such an entity that provides counseling with a narrow scope, especially not covering at least all three areas specified in art. 3a sec. 1 the second sentence, UNPP, will not be a non-governmental organization specified in art. 11b para. 2 UNPP. This is indirectly indicated in the elements of the content of training and supplementary courses conducted by the entity authorized under art. 11b para. 2 UNPP. These elements were set out in art. 11a para. 1 the first sentence and art. 2 the second sentence of UNPP, under which: "the minimum scope of the training includes 70 hours of civic counseling classes, of which at least 15 hours are spent on counseling methodology and at least 20 hours in counseling for indebted people"; "the supplementary course includes at least 8 hours of classes in the field of practical aspects related to the provision of civic counseling, including its specific areas". The content of these provisions strongly suggests that the civic counseling (as a condition for obtaining the appropriate authorization – art. 11b (1) and (2) UNPP) practiced by the entity providing the above-mentioned training must reach out beyond a single area, including, inter alia, advice for indebted persons (see art. 11a (1) the first sentence and art. 3a (1) the second sentence of the UNPP).

5. Conclusions

The analysis appears to provide sufficient grounds to assume the following constatations.

The concept "civic counseling", presented in the form of either "non-adjective" or bearing the adjective "free-of-charge", should be understood – in terms of features, types and subject of activities uniformly throughout the Act and reduced to the meaning resulting from art. 3a UNPP. This conclusion is justified in particular by the: results of the application of the so-called terminological consequence directive, the formulation of the definition in art. 3a of the UNPP omitting the explanation of the term "free of charge" and the purposeful aspects of the analyzed provisions of the UNPP.

Civic counseling is an activity that fulfills cumulatively the conditions set out in art. 3a sec. 1 the first sentence and art. 2 of the UNPP, differentiated in terms of subject matter – concerning at least all of the areas specified in art. 3a sec. 1 the second sentence, UNPP. Support for such a conclusion can be sought in studies of the normative contexts of the use of the discussed concept in individual provisions of the UNPP, especially in art. 11a para. the first sentence 1 and art. 2 the second sentence (indicating the scope of training and supplementary courses for counselors) and Art. 8a sec. 1 UNPP (differentiating civic counseling and counseling in specific, individual areas).

Given the rather vague formation of art. 3a of the UNPP, specifying the meaning of the term "civil counseling" should also take place from the negative side, by distinguishing it from providing legal assistance within the meaning of art. 3 of the UNPP, providing legal advice and information, providing legal education (art. 3b UNPP), as well as advising on specialized areas (see art. 8a (1) (1) UNPP). This assumption is consequential on the prohibition on synonymous interpretation, according to which different terms of the legal language should not be granted the same meaning.

At the same time, it must be stressed that the introduction in art. 3a of the UNPP of the definition of "civic counseling" is normatively justified due to the need to precisely define the extent of implementation of specific legal obligations provided for in the provisions of UNPP. This is closely related to the need for: (1) sound assessment of the correct performance of the public task consisting in providing free-of-charge civic counseling; (2) establishing the competence of the persons mentioned in art. 11 sec. 3a UNPP; (3) designating the subject of training and supplementary courses for counselors; (4) indication of the entity authorized to conduct such trainings and courses.

The analysis appears to justify the thesis that since art. 3a of the UNPP contains a general and open definition of "civic counseling", decoding its meaning under the provisions of the UNPP requires also referring to the normative context of its use in a number of other provisions of this Act, including a comparison with the terms "synonymous" relating to legal support for the poor (which emphasizes the special role of the systemic and purposeful interpretation of the examined regulations).

Literature

B.a., *System nieodpłatnego poradnictwa prawnego i obywatelskiego w Polsce*, Warszawa 2013.

Bartnik A. S., Kowalska K. J., *Poradnictwo prawne i obywatelskie w kontekście świadomości prawnej i potrzeby edukacji prawnej Polaków. Wybrane problemy*, „Studia Iuridica" 2018, nr LXXVIII.

Chauvin T., Stawecki T., Winczorek P., Wstęp do prawoznawstwa, Warszawa 2016.

Henning I., *O poradnictwie prawnym i obywatelskim*, [w:] I. Henning, A. Rozkosz (eds.), *Poradnik dla doradczyń i doradców poradnictwa prawnego i obywatelskiego*, Warszawa 2014.

Jarra E., *Ogólna teorja prawa*, Warszawa 1922.

Morawski L., *Zasady wykładni prawa*, Toruń 2006.

Parlicki M., *Poradnictwo obywatelskie jako aktywizacyjna forma pomocy oferowana jednostkom i rodzinom*, „Państwo i Społeczeństwo" 2012, nr 4.

Przywora B., Wróbel A., *Poradnictwo obywatelskie w świetle badań prawnoporównawczych*, Warszawa 2020, https://iws.gov.pl/wp-content/uploads/2021/01/IWS_Przywora-B.-Wr%C3%B3bel-A._Poradnictwo-obywatelskie-w-%C5%9Bwietle-bada%C5%84-prawnopor%C3%B3wnawczych.pdf; (accessed: 20.01.2021).

Schimanek T., Wiaderek G., *Poradnictwo prawne i obywatelskie – pojęcie, jakość, efektywność*, [w:] *Czym jest poradnictwo prawne i obywatelskie*, Warszawa 2011.

Ziembiński Z., *Logika praktyczna*, Warszawa 1997. Źródła internetowe.

Michał Czerniawski

The professional secrecy obligation of the legal profession in Poland and the General Data Protection Regulation

Abstract: The chapter discusses the impact of data protection laws on providing legal advice, including free legal aid, in Poland. It scrutinizes national provisions based on derogations foreseen in the General Data Protection Regulation, particularly concerning the relationship between the right to the protection of personal data and an obligation of professional secrecy of advocates and attorneys-at-law. In its second part, the article discusses the powers of the Polish data protection authority concerning advocates and attorneys-at-law processing personal data to provide legal advice. In the chapter, the author argues that the Polish legislator correctly implemented relevant derogations provided for in the GDPR and that the limitations to the rights of data subjects envisaged in the Polish law fulfil the requirements set in the EU law.

Keywords: legal aid, personal data protection, professional secrecy

1. Introduction

The GDPR applies to the processing of personal data wholly or partly by automated means and to the processing other than by automated means of personal data, which form part of a filing system or are intended to form part of a filing system.[1] Processing of data under the GDPR means any operation or set of operations, which is performed on personal data or sets of personal data, whether or not by automated means, such as collection, recording, organization, structuring, storage, adaptation or alteration, retrieval, consultation, use, disclosure by transmission, dissemination or otherwise making available, alignment or combination, restriction, erasure or destruction.

---

1 See Art. 2 of Regulation (EU) 2016/679 of the European Parliament and of the Council of 27 April 2016 on the protection of natural persons with regard to the processing of personal data and on the free movement of such data, and repealing Directive 95/46/EC (General Data Protection Regulation) [2016] Official Journal of the European Union L119/1 – 88.

Every lawyer providing legal assistance, including free legal aid, at some point will process personal data and will be obliged to apply data protection laws. At the same time, the GDPR provides for several exceptions from its scope of application. For example, an exception that may apply in the day-to-day work of a lawyer is the processing of personal data by a natural person as part of a purely personal or household activity, listed in art. 2.2.(c) GDPR.[2]

After it was adopted, in order to align national laws with the GDPR, the Polish legislator adopted two legal acts: (i) the Polish Data Protection Act;[3] and (ii) the Act on the amendments of some legal acts in connection with the implementation of the GDPR.[4] The first act implemented the GDPR into the Polish legal order, and the latter amended over 160 Polish sectoral acts, including those that regulate the professions of attorneys-at-law and advocates.

2. Providing legal aid and the GDPR

Providing legal advice, generally, involves obtaining information about an identified or identifiable natural person, i.e., personal data within the meaning of the GDPR. In the course of providing legal assistance, lawyers usually process three categories of data: (i) clients' data – these are usually their names, surnames, addresses of residence or correspondence; (ii) data of witnesses, experts and other participants in the proceedings – i.e. data of various persons related to the case, (iii) information about the case itself – e.g. case numbers that in certain situations may also constitute personal data.

2.1 Lawyer - a controller or a processor?

With respect to roles and responsibilities, the European Union's data protection laws introduce a model that should be qualified as "binary": one who processes

---

2 Therefore, the provisions on the protection of personal data will not apply, for example, when the processing of personal data by an attorney-at-law or an advocate is performed for purely private purposes, e.g., when sending Christmas cards to their clients. In Recital 18 GDPR, the EU legislator specifies that a purely personal or household activity is an activity that has no connection to a professional or commercial activity. According to the same recital, "personal or household activities could include correspondence and the holding of addresses, or social networking and online activity undertaken within the context of such activities". The GDPR does not make any clear distinction regarding a profit- or non-profit nature of processing; however, any kind of gainful activity should be considered as outside the scope of "purely personal or household activity".

3 Act of 10 May 2018 on the Protection of Personal Data (Journal of Laws of 2019, item 1781).

4 Act of 21 February 2019 on the amendments of some legal acts in connection with the implementation of the GDPR (Journal of Laws of 2019, item 730).

personal data may be either a controller (including a joint controller) or a processor. The EU co-legislators have not foreseen any other category of entities that may be involved in the processing of personal data. A controller means "the natural or legal person, public authority, agency or other body which, alone or jointly with others, determines the purposes and means of the processing of personal data". Controllers shoulder the highest level of compliance responsibility – they must comply with a significant number of obligations as set in the GDPR. They are also responsible for the GDPR compliance of any processors they might use to process the data. In case of violation of law, they are subject to severe administrative fines. On the other hand, a processor, processes personal data only on behalf of a controller, i.e., not in an independent manner, therefore it is subject to much fewer obligations than a controller, and to much more limited liability. For this reason, many entities would prefer to act as processors rather than controllers. In this context, it should be underlined that providing legal aid by an attorney-at-law or an advocate requires independent decision-making without being obliged to execute instructions from a client. Therefore, in general, lawyers providing legal advice should be considered as controllers. Finally, there is no doubt that lawyers acting in their professional capacity have the status of a controller in so far as they process the personal data of their employees, permanent collaborators, trainees, occasional collaborators (e.g., notaries public, sworn interpreters or other lawyers), suppliers of goods and services (natural persons carrying out an economic activity), etc.

2.2. Obligation of professional secrecy under the Polish law

Polish law does not provide for a legal definition of professional secrecy. This term can be understood as an obligation of confidentiality arising from the exercise of a profession identified as a profession of public trust. Public trust professions, including attorneys-at-law and advocates, cannot function without confidentiality. An obligation of secrecy guarantees trust towards lawyers and protects the otherwise vulnerable relationship between a lawyer and a client. The exact scope of professional secrecy is usually determined by relevant sectoral laws and, in addition, by the legal professions' codes of ethics. It consists of the legal and the ethical layers. However, the sole fact that attorneys-at-law and advocates are bound by the obligation of professional secrecy (as a principle, covering everything they have learned in the course of their professional activities) does not exempt them from their obligations applicable under other laws, including data protection laws.

Under Polish law, the legal basis for attorneys-at-law and advocates' professional secrecy obligation can be found in generally applicable law and relevant codes of ethics. The Attorneys at Law Act[5] in art. 3(3) states that an attorney-at-law shall maintain the secrecy of any information acquired in connection with providing legal assistance. This obligation may not be limited in time. In addition, an

5 The Attorneys at Law Act of 6 July 1982 (Journal of Laws 2020, item 75).

attorney-at-law may not be exempted from the obligation of professional secrecy with regard to facts of which he has become aware by providing legal aid, except information falling within the scope of the anti-money laundering and terrorist financing laws[6] as well as in relation to hearings in tax cases to the extent specified in the tax legislation.

In line with Article 6 of the law of the Advocates' Profession,[7] a similar obligation of professional secrecy applies to advocates. Under this act, an advocate is obliged to maintain the confidentiality of everything they learnt while providing legal assistance. The duty to keep professional secrets cannot be limited in time. Finally, advocates may not be relieved from their duty to maintain professional secrets with regard to facts that came to their knowledge while providing legal assistance or handling a case. Similarly to the attorneys-at-laws' duties, this is with the exception of information falling within the scope of the anti-money laundering and terrorist financing laws[8] as well as in relation to hearings in tax cases to the extent specified in the tax legislation.

As I have already mentioned, both attorneys-at-law and advocates are obliged not only to act in accordance with laws regulating their professions, but also to adhere to strict ethical principles (see respectively art. 64(1) of the Attorneys at Law Act and art. 80 of the law of the Advocates' Profession). The scope of the obligation of secrecy is further specified in relevant codes of ethics. For example, art. 15 of the Attorneys at Law Code of Ethics provides that an attorney-at-law must keep confidential all information relating to the client and his affairs disclosed to the attorney- at-law by the client or otherwise obtained in the course of the performance of any professional activity, regardless of the source of the information and the form and manner in which it is recorded. Violation of these rules can result in disciplinary liability.

The topic of professional secrets is also regulated by national data protection laws. The Polish Act on the amendments of some legal acts in connection with the implementation of the GDPR stipulates that the provisions regarding the right of access by a data subject (including the right to obtain a copy of data undergoing processing, i.e. art. 15 (1) and (3) GDPR), right to restriction of processing (art. 18 GDPR), as well as the notification obligations regarding rectification or erasure of personal data or restriction of processing (art. 19 GDPR) shall apply to the extent that they do not violate the attorney-at law's or advocate's obligation to maintain professional secrecy. Concerning the right to object to the processing of data (art. 21 GDPR), this right does not apply to personal data obtained by an attorney-at-law or an advocate in connection with providing legal aid.

6 Act of 16 November 2000 on Counteracting Money Laundering and Terrorism Financing (Journal of Laws of 2017, item 1049 as amended).

7 The law of the Advocates' Profession of 26 May 1982 (Journal of Laws 2020 item 1651).

8 Act of 16th November 2000 on Counteracting Money Laundering and Terrorism Financing (Journal of Laws of 2017, item 1049 as amended).

2.3. Obligation of professional secrecy under the GDPR

In the GDPR, the EU co-legislators decided to take into account the specific nature of certain professions, which are bound by the obligation of professional secrecy and allowed the possibility to restrict the application of some of its provisions on the grounds of the protection of such secrecy and professional ethics. This obligation may, therefore, constitute grounds for limiting or excluding the application of specific provisions of the GDPR, including the provisions on data subjects' rights.

Art. 14(5)(d) GDPR explicitly states that the obligation to provide information when personal data is obtained not from a data subject will not apply in situations where personal data must remain confidential subject to an obligation of professional secrecy regulated by Union or Member State law. An attorney-at-law or an advocate bound by a statutory obligation of secrecy is therefore exempted from the obligation to inform a data subject in situations where they have obtained personal data indirectly. For example, if an attorney-at-law or an advocate has acquired personal data of a witness or another party to the proceedings not from the witness or the party (but, e.g. from a client or publicly accessible registers), the lawyer does not have to comply with the information duty arising from art. 14 GDPR.

Union or Member State law may also limit the right of access by a data subject to their data. One of the grounds for such a limitation may be an adverse effect on the rights and freedoms of others. For example, insofar as an attorney-at-law or an advocate is subject to professional secrecy, if a third party (e.g. a defendant) requests, based on art. 15 GDPR, information about the processing of their personal data or a copy of their personal data, an attorney-at-law or an advocate should refuse to disclose that information or a copy. In such a case, it is enough to justify the refusal by the right of the client to keep their data processed by their lawyer and related to their case confidential.

2.4. Professional secrecy and supervision over the processing of personal data

According to art. 58(1)(e)(f) GDPR, among other powers, each supervisory authority has the investigative power to obtain, from a controller or a processor, access to all personal data and all information necessary for the performance of its tasks and to obtain access to any premises of a controller or a processor, including to any data processing equipment or other means, in accordance with Union or national procedural laws. These powers are, however, subject to limitations foreseen in art. 90 GDPR. In line with this provision, Member States may adopt specific rules to set out the powers of the supervisory authorities in relation to controllers or processors that are subject, under Union or Member State law or rules established by national competent bodies, to an obligation of professional secrecy or other equivalent obligations of secrecy. Such rules may be adopted where it is necessary and proportionate to reconcile the right to protect personal data with the obligation of secrecy. These limitations shall apply only to personal data that a controller or a processor has received as a result of or has obtained in an activity covered by that obligation of secrecy. As pointed out by W. Svanberg, this provision must be interpreted in light of the relevant CJEU case law, the Charter of Fundamental Rights and art. 16(2) of the Treaty on the Functioning of the European Union.[9] The CJEU case law that deals with the independence of supervisory authorities includes in particular, Case C-518/07 Commission v Germany,[10] Case C-614/10 Commission v Austria[11] and case C-288/12 Commission v Hungary.[12] According to Art. 90(2) GDPR, each Member State had to notify the European Commission of any relevant national laws by 25 May 2018 and, without delay, should notify any subsequent amendments affecting them. Restrictions under art.

9 See W. Svanberg, Commentary to art. 90 GDPR, [in:] Ch. Kuner, L. A. Bygrave, C. Docksey (eds.), The EU General Data Protection Regulation (GDPR): A Commentary, p. 1255.

10 Judgment of the Court (Grand Chamber) of 9 March 2010 in Case C-518/07, European Commission, supported by European Data Protection Supervisor v Federal Republic of Germany. In this case, the Court found that supervisory authorities responsible for supervising the processing of personal data outside the public sector must enjoy independence, allowing them to perform their duties free from external influence. Such independence precludes not only any influence exercised by the supervised bodies, but also any directions or any other external influence, whether direct or indirect, which could call into question the performance by those authorities of their tasks. The mere risk that the scrutinizing authorities could exercise a political influence over the decisions of the competent supervisory authorities is enough to hinder the supervisory authorities' independent performance of their tasks. State scrutiny of national supervisory authorities is not, therefore, compatible with the requirement of independence.

11 Judgment of the Court (Grand Chamber) in Case C-614/10 of 16 October 2012 European Commission v Republic of Austria. According to the judgement, the Member State which lays down a regulatory framework under which the supervisory authority's managing member is a federal official subject to supervision, and his office is integrated with national government departments, including that the head of the national government has an unconditional right to information covering all aspects of that authority's work, does not meet the requirement of independence of a supervisory authority. The independence required in such relation is intended to preclude direct influence, in the form of instructions, and any indirect influence, which may affect the supervisory authority's decisions.

12 Judgment of the Court (Grand Chamber) in Case C-288/12, 8 April 2014 European Commission v Hungary. In this case, the Court stated that a supervisory authority responsible for supervising the processing of personal data must enjoy independence, allowing it to perform its duties free from external influence in whatever form, whether direct or indirect, which may have an effect on its decisions and which could call in question the performance by the authority of its tasks. The mere risk that state scrutinising authority could exercise political influence over the decisions of such supervisory authority is enough to hinder the latter in the independent performance of its tasks.

90 GDPR apply to attorneys-at-law and advocates acting both as controllers or processors. At the same time, it should be noted that when an attorney-at-law or an advocate acts as a processor and refuses to hand over personal data to the supervisory authority, the authority may still attempt to obtain data from a controller or other entities that have access to it and which may not be subject the same confidentiality obligations.

The fact that data is covered by the obligation of professional secrecy does prevent a data protection authority from verifying the compliance of a controller or a processor, who is an attorney-at-law or an advocate, with the GDPR obligations in relation to such data. The supervisory authority can still check, e.g., the security of the data, including technical and organizational measures put in place to ensure GDPR compliance – however, such actions can be taken only without obtaining access to the content of the data itself. Personal data that is not subject to the obligation of professional secrecy may be subject to investigation and access by the authority without any restrictions. The Polish supervisory authority may, therefore, obtain access, for example, to the personal data of individuals employed by a particular advocate or attorney-at-law. To summarize, it should be underlined that the Polish law, as a principle, confirms the primacy of professional secrecy over the prerogatives of the data protection authority. The obligation of professional secrecy cannot be limited in any way – professional secrecy covers all documents created by an attorney-at-law or an advocate, including correspondence with the client or other persons involved in the case in connection with it, as well as any information disclosed to the lawyer before they started their actions.

3. Conclusion

A lawyer providing legal assistance, including free legal advice, is obliged to apply the GDPR and in most cases should be considered a controller, subject to relevant responsibilities, such as the obligation to provide information, grant access to data or provide its copy to a data subject. At the same time, professions such as attorney-at-law or advocate rely on a special relationship of trust between a lawyer and his client. The Polish legislator regulated the correlation between the right to the protection of personal data and an obligation of professional secrecy of attorneys-at-law and advocates by applying derogations from general data protection rules as foreseen in the GDPR. These exceptions enable attorneys-at-law and advocates to provide legal assistance in an independent manner and ensure that information about their clients and their cases is protected. The Polish legislator implemented these derogations into the Polish legal order correctly, and all the limitations to the rights of data subjects, who are not clients, as well as to investigative powers of the supervisory authority linked to the obligation of secrecy, have been introduced taking into due account the requirements defined by the EU law.

Literature

Ch. Kuner, L.A. Bygrave, Ch. Docksey, *The EU General Data Protection Regulation (GDPR). A commentary*, Oxford 2020.

Olgierd Kucharski[1]

Free legal aid provided by National Labour Inspectorate

Abstract: The aim of the study is to characterize the free legal aid provided by the National Labor Inspectorate within its statutory competences. In analyzing the aspect of the system of providing free legal aid in Poland to obtain the whole picture, we should also take into account the activity of various administrative bodies in this field. The research portion of the study was based on statistical data from 2014 to 2018. An analysis of the quantity and structure of the advice given was presented. Provision of advice by this authority does not depend on the criterion of the beneficiary's financial situation. The National Labor Inspectorate, as a body involved in the supervision and control in the area of labor law and legality of employment, plays a prominent role in this field due to the large number of people performing work and offering employment, and therefore seeking expertise about legal standards in this area.

Keywords: National Labor Inspectorate, free legal counseling

1. Introduction

The necessity to provide free legal aid to people who, for various reasons, cannot use professional legal services in a democratic state under the rule of law should not raise any controversies. The *Ignorantia iuris nocet* and *Ignorantia iuris non excusat* principles cause those various legal sanctions, as well as other adverse effects of the lack of legal knowledge, can affect any legal entity. In such situations, evoking ignorance of the law is not an effective measure to exclude liability. These premises arising directly from the provisions of art. 2 and 83 of the Constitution RP form the basis for the organization of the free legal aid system. This is an interesting issue in itself and the subject of scientific reflection[2]. There is also a statute that regulates the issues of providing free legal aid. However, it is not the objective

---

1 Jan Długosz University in Częstochowa. ORCID: 0000-0002-9633-9281.
2 B. Przywora, *Normatywny model przedsądowej nieodpłatnej pomocy prawne w Polsce*, Warsaw 2019.

of this paper to reconstruct the values underlying the legal solutions for such activities in Poland or to analyze the provisions of the Free Legal Aid Act.

The intention of this chapter is to characterize principles of granting free legal aid provided by one of the state institutions, namely the National Labour Inspectorate. The need to provide information on the subject-matter jurisdiction is, as a rule, the obligation of administrative authorities, resulting from the provisions on administrative proceedings[3]. Such actions are generally free of charge (with the exception of certain legal interpretations). Therefore, when analyzing the issue of the system of providing free legal aid in Poland, one should also consider the activities of various administrative bodies, including the National Labour Inspectorate, in this regard to get the whole picture.

2. The issue of the flow of information on applicable laws and regulations

The basic assumption of a democratic state under the rule of law is the knowledge of legal norms by the entities concerned because it is a necessary condition for these rules to influence their behavior[4]. However, it is also commonly known that the assumption of the common legal knowledge is a counterfactual assumption albeit necessary to be able to use a legal sanction in all cases where violations of the law are associated with the lack of knowledge about (or, more broadly, awareness of) the content of applicable legal regulations[5]. It gives rise to the question of where citizens learn about the law.

Communication processes disseminating information about the law were characterized by Franciszek Studnicki almost 50 years ago[6]. If follows from his findings that it is possible to distinguish seven types of communication processes thanks to which the addressee receives messages about the law[7]:

1. processes in which the addressee obtains knowledge from official publications (*Journal of Laws, Monitor Polski*);
2. processes in which the addressee receives news about the law directly from the mass media (the press, radio, television and, currently, primarily, the Internet);
3. processes in which the addressee gets information from sources other than those indicated above (such as school, training);

3 Which follows from art. 9 Administrative Procedure Code.
4 A. Redelbach, S. Wronkowska, Z. Ziembiński, *Zarys teorii państwa i prawa*, Warsaw 1994, p. 235.
5 J. Kowalski, W. Lamentowicz, P. Winczorek, *Teoria państwa i prawa*, Warsaw 1981, pp. 209–210.
6 F. Studnicki, *Cybernetyka i prawo*, Warsaw 1969; F. Studnicki, *Przepływ wiadomości o normach prawa*, Zeszyty Naukowe UJ, Prace prawnicze 22/1965.
7 F. Studnicki, Przepływ..., pp. 64–65.

4. processes in which it receives information about the law as contained in individual decisions concerning that addressee (such as judgments, administrative decisions);
5. processes in which the addressee receives information while participating in making official decisions (for example, as a lay judge, councilor, MP, senator);
6. processes in which the addressee receives information by contacting legal experts (such as attorneys-at-law, legal advisers, officials);
7. processes in which the addressee receives information during interpersonal contacts (with their family, friends, colleagues).

Regardless of the assessment of which source is the most effective in providing information, it should be noted that due to the enormous number of legal provisions and their constant variability, it is impossible to know all of them; therefore, there is a need to constantly increase knowledge in this regard.

It seems that official publications are a source of knowledge about legal standards only for people professionally involved in law application processes (judges, attorneys-at-law, legal advisers, notaries, clerks, etc.). The language of legal instruments is very formalized and specific, and the variability of legal texts often makes it impossible to find an instrument in its current wording (official publications usually contain amendments to legal texts rather than uniform texts). This is why other communication processes providing knowledge about the applicable law play a very important role in the case of other entities.

In particular, this applies to knowledge about legal norms obtained from legal experts, which has such an advantage over other sources that the information obtained in this way also contain, apart from messages about the content of the law, authoritative knowledge about the practice of applying legal norms supported by experience. An additional advantage is the ability to adjust the form and content of the information to the state of consciousness of the person seeking advice, which, unfortunately, cannot be done in the mass media. This makes expert advice very popular, especially when provided free of charge.

This group of sources on the content of the law includes free expert advice provided by administrative bodies, including the National Labour Inspectorate[8].

Free legal aid should provide access to the highest level of knowledge about laws and regulations and, simultaneously, for the greatest possible number of people who, for various reasons, don't use payable expert advice. Without going into too much detail about these complex issues, which are not the subject matter of this paper, I would just like to emphasize that the state's duty to take action aimed at providing knowledge about the law to the widest possible group of citizens results from the principles of operation of a democratic state under the rule of law.

---

8 D. Makowski, *Inspekcja Pracy jako instytucja państwowego nadzoru nad przestrzeganiem prawa pracy*, Łódź 2017, p. 181 et seq.

3. Free legal aid in the area of labor law

Free legal aid in the area of labor law, including occupational health and safety and legality of employment, is particularly important as the employment market consists of over 13 million employees, not including the entities that employ them[9]. Not all of these people may, in a given situation, use payable legal assistance. There are various reasons for this state of affairs; the following ones can be indicated in a way that does not aspire to exhaust the issue: financial reasons, a low level of legal awareness and culture, the lack of availability of law offices in every place, the need to obtain the necessary advice quickly (which is possible thanks to advice provided by phone), and, finally, the technical nature of some of the provisions of labor law (for example, how the holiday pay is calculated or how personal files and other documentation on the employment relationship should be kept). Anticipating the subsequent findings, I would like to point out that as regards labor law issues, advice is often requested by employers or people who provide HR and payroll services, therefore, who usually have a higher than average level of legal knowledge, but who don't always want to use professional legal services even with respect to very important issues (such as concluding non-competition agreements, termination of employment contracts in disputed cases), which, unfortunately, proves the still low level of legal culture. It is still not a universal rule that an entity running a business should also constantly cooperate with a professional law firm, an attorney-at-law, or a legal adviser. Regardless of the reasons, administrative bodies should take action within the scope of their competence to raise the level of knowledge about legal regulations.

As a result, the role of free advice provided by a specialized body controlling and supervising the compliance with labor law and legality of employment, which is the National Labour Inspectorate, becomes very important[10].

The obligation to provide free advice within the body's subject-matter competence is stipulated directly in art. 10(7)(e) of the said Act, and it follows from this article that this institution's responsibilities include taking action to prevent and reduce risks in the work environment, in particular, by providing advice on how to reduce threats to employees' life and health, as well as on the compliance with labor laws and regulations. The scope of advice specified in the Act applies to the entire subject-matter jurisdiction of the authority. As a result, certain organizational resources have been allocated to meet this obligation, in particular, by

9 According to data from https://rynekpracy.org/statystyki/liczba-pracujacych/ (accessed: 15.11.2020). On the page of this website, it is stated that the number of people employed in Poland is over 16 million (which includes all employees, regardless of the basis of employment, as well as people working in their own or leased farms, sole traders, and people cooperating with them); at least 80 % of them perform contract work, thus, over 13 million people.

10 The Act of 13 April 2007 on the National Labour Inspectorate (Journal of Laws of 2019, item 1251).

offering telephone and written advice, as well as oral advice at the units' headquarters. In connection with the idea of unifying the rules for providing advice, the Counseling Centre operating at the Chief Labour Inspectorate in Warsaw was launched in 2018, which mainly provides advice by phone. To a large extent, it has taken over the task of providing advice by phone, which was previously provided entirely by district labor inspectorates, and now is only provided on certain days of a week.

Regardless of this provision, it should be indicated that authorities of the National Labour Inspectorate, namely labor inspectors, are required to provide legal information (which also forms *de facto* and *de jure* free legal assistance) during performed inspection activities. It follows from art. 12 of the said Act, which stipulates that the provisions of the Administrative Procedure Code shall apply to unregulated matters in proceedings before the authorities of the National Labour Inspectorate. This makes it necessary to comply with art. 9 of that Code, which requires public administration bodies to properly and fully inform the parties about the factual and legal circumstances that may affect the determination of their rights and obligations being the subject of administrative proceedings. The authorities are also required to ensure that the parties and other persons participating in administrative proceedings don't suffer damage because of the ignorance of the law, and to this end, they provide the parties with necessary explanations and instructions.

Therefore, the indicated provisions constitute the legal basis for the right but also the obligation of the National Labour Inspectorate's employees to provide free advice within its subject-matter competence. This also means that when providing legal advice, no criterion is applied; in particular, it is not examined whether the applicant is unable to bear costs of payable legal assistance.

4. The National Labour Inspectorate

Before presenting a statistical analysis of the advice provided, it is necessary to note the possible scope and complexity of the issues it covers. The National Labour Inspectorate is an authority established to supervise and control the compliance with labor law, in particular, the provisions on and principles of occupational health and safety, as well as provisions on the legality of employment and other gainful work to the extent specified in the Act[11].

When presenting the scope of advice provided by the National Labour Inspectorate, which is necessary to draw attention to the considerable size and complexity of its subject area, attention should be paid, first of all, to the provisions of the Labour Code[12]. The provisions it includes constitute the basis of labor law. In

11 Art. 1 of the Act of 13 April 2007 on the National Labour Inspectorate.
12 The Act of 26 June 1974 – Labour Code (Journal of Laws of 2020, item 1320).

particular, one can indicate the following groups of issues it regulates, which are covered by counseling:

(a) In-house labor law regulations and their semi-compulsory nature;
(b) Employment relationship – its establishment and termination, where more important groups of topics can be distinguished:
  - forms of employment and types of employment contracts;
  - conclusion and content of an employment contract, protection of personal data;
  - termination of employment contracts and employment certificates.
(c) Remuneration and other benefits, and related groups of issues:
  - remuneration systems, allowances, equivalents, severance pays, compensations;
  - calculation of wages, allowances, and equivalents – regulated by intricate and detailed implementing regulations;[13]
  - protection of remuneration for work;
(d) Working time and issues related to it:
  - standards, full-time equivalents, systems, schedules, organization of working time, settlement periods;
  - obligatory rests;
  - overtime hours and their norms, methods of compensation;
  - work at night, on Sundays and public holidays.
(e) Annual leaves – time dimensions, rules for granting.
(f) Disciplinary responsibility.
(g) Material responsibility.
(h) Obligations of employers and employees, including in terms of:
  - employee documentation and the period of its storage;
  - records of hours worked and justification of absences.
(i) Parental rights.
(j) Employment of young people.
(k) Equal treatment in employment. Mobbing.
(l) Occupational health and safety and resulting issues:
  - health and safety obligations of employers, employees, and people managing employees;

13 Regulation of the Minister of Labour and Social Policy of 8 January 1997 on detailed rules for granting an annual leave, determining and paying remuneration for the leave and cash equivalent for the leave (Journal of Laws of 1997, No. 2, item 14); Regulation of the Minister of Labour and Social Policy of 29 May 1996 on the method of determining remuneration during a period of without performing work and remuneration forming the basis for calculating compensations, severance pays, compensatory supplements to the remuneration and other amounts due provided for in the Labour Code (Journal of Laws of 2017, item 927).

- technical work safety, including buildings and workrooms, machinery and equipment for production processes, harmful factors, preventive health protection, training;
- accidents at work, occupational diseases, which are additionally regulated by numerous detailed implementing instruments.

Moreover, apart from the Labour Code, it is possible to designate statutes that define the rights and obligations of employees falling under the supervision of the National Labour Inspectorate:

(a) Regulations on drivers' working hours;[14]
(b) Regulations on collective redundancies;[15]

Moreover, it is necessary to indicate statues that belong to the above group, in the case of which, only recently, there have been numerous changes or completely new employment regulations have entered into force, concerning, for example:

(a) Ban on trading on Sundays and public holidays;[16]
(b) Provisions on minimum wage (commissions);[17]
(c) Legality of employment, including foreigners;[18]
(d) Regulations on Employee Capital Programmes[19]

This non-exhaustive catalogue is to indicate the broad scope of the subject-matter competence of the National Labour Inspectorate, and thus the free advice provided. On the other hand, most of the issues on which advice is provided are generally of a non-controversial or even technical nature when it comes to indicating, for example, working time standards or time dimensions of annual leaves, methods of calculating wages, and other benefits from employment relationships. This applies not only to employees, but also to HR and payroll services and small employers.

14 The Act of 16 April 2004 on Drivers' Working Hours (Journal of Laws of 2019, item 1412).
15 The Act of 13 March 2003 on Special Rules for Terminating Employment Relationships with Employees for Reasons Not Attributable to Employees (Journal of Laws of 2018, item 1969).
16 Act of 10 January 2018 on Restrictions on Trade on Sundays, Public Holidays and Certain Days (Journal of Laws of 2018, item 305).
17 The Act of 10 October 2002 on Minimum Wage (Journal of Laws of 2018, item 2177).
18 the Act of 20 April 2004 on Promotion of Employment and Labour Market Institutions (Journal of Laws of 2020, item 1409).
19 the Act of 4 October 2018 on Employee Capital Programmes (Journal of Laws of 2018, item 2215).

5. A statistical summary of advice provided by the National Labour Inspectorate

A statistical summary of advice provided by the National Labour Inspectorate in 2014 and 2018 will be presented[20]. This will allow one to capture general dependencies resulting from the summary.

In 2014, employees of the National Labour Inspectorate provided a total of 1.2 million free consultations[21].

In terms of the content, consultations can be divided into advice on strictly legal topics related to employment and technical safety at work, thus, the issues regulated by Section X of the Labour Code concerning occupational health and safety and instruments implementing these provisions. In this respect, the following advice was provided, respectively:

- 939,000 consultations on legal issues related to labor protection;
- 260,000 consultations on technical issues of occupational health and safety.

At the headquarters of organizational units of the National Labour Inspectorate, 725,000 oral consultations and 50,000 phone consultations were provided.

During inspection activities, labor inspectors provided 214,000 consultations on strictly legal topics and 210,000 consultations on technical safety at work, respectively.

The people who asked for advice were:

- employees – 50.6 %,
- employers and people acting on their behalf (people from HR and accounting departments, etc.) – 27 %
- former employees – 13 %,
- other people, including social labor inspectors, individual farmers, persons providing OHS services – 8.8 %,
- representatives of trade unions – 0.6 %.

In terms of the content of the advice provided, it concerned:

- 28.4 % – entering into and terminating an employment relationship;
- 18.2 % – remuneration;
- 11.3 % – working time;
- 8.8 % – holidays;
- 7.5 % – parentage;
- 5.1 % – working conditions;

---

20 It follows, for example, from the fact that more recent reports are unavailable, and that the amount of provided advice was not reported in 2016 and 2017.

21 https://www.pip.gov.pl/pl/o-urzedzie/sprawozdania-z-dzialalnosci/archiwum/2014 (accessed: 5.11.2020).

- 2.3 % – legality of employment;
- 1.4 % – accidents at work;
- 1.2 % – collective labor agreements;
- 0.8 % – discrimination and mobbing;
- 15 % – other.

In 2018, employees of the National Labour Inspectorate provided a total of 740,000 free consultations.[22]

In terms of the content, consultations can be divided into advice on strictly legal topics related to employment and technical safety at work, thus, the issues regulated by Section X of the Labour Code concerning occupational health and safety and instruments implementing these provisions. In this respect, the following advice was provided, respectively:

- 540,000 consultations on legal issues related to labor protection;
- 200,000 consultations on technical issues of occupational health and safety.

At the headquarters of organizational units of the National Labour Inspectorate, 395,000 consultations were provided, of which 197,000 were consultations provided at the Counseling Centre, which started its operations and began taking over advice provided by phone from district labor inspectorates in 2018.

During inspection activities, labor inspectors provided 344,000 consultations, which included more than 161,000 consultations on technical safety at work, over 151,000 consultations on strictly legal employment issues, and more than 31,000 consultations on the legality of employment.

In 2018, the report showed that at the offices of the Inspectorate, 56.1 % of consultations were provided by phone, 40 % – in person, 3.2 % – in writing, and 0.7 % via e-mail.

The people who asked for advice were:

- employees – 49 %,
- employers and people acting on their behalf (people from HR and accounting departments, etc.) – 27 %
- former employees – 12.9 %,
- other people, including social labor inspectors, individual farmers, persons providing OHS services, foreigners – 10.7 %,
- representatives of trade unions – 0.4 %.

In terms of the content of the advice provided, it concerned:

- 36 % – entering into and terminating an employment relationship;
- 16 % – remuneration;

22 https://www.pip.gov.pl/pl/o-urzedzie/sprawozdania-z-dzialalnosci/archiwum/2018 (accessed: 5.11.2020).

- 10 % – working time;
- 8 % – holidays;
- 6 % – parentage;
- 6 % – occupational health and safety;
- 18 % – other.

The report also indicates that in the years 2017–2018, there were major changes in the labor law as regards the ban on trading on Sundays and public holidays, employee documentation and fixed-term employment contracts, and parentage protection; moreover, employees hired under commission contracts were covered by the minimum wage protection.

Employees of the Counseling Centre reported that in most cases, people seeking advice by phone were characterized by high legal awareness, and the questions asked were specific and detailed. It could be related to the fact that people specializing in HR and accounting issues often asked for advice.

6. Conclusions

Free legal counseling is essential in any democratic state. This issue also applies to administrative bodies which provide free and necessary legal information within the scope of their subject-matter competence to all interested entities, without using the beneficiary's financial standing as the criterion for providing assistance.

The National Labour Inspectorate, as a body responsible for supervision and control in the area of labor law and legality of employment, plays a significant role in this field because of the large number of people who employ and are employed and, therefore, seek knowledge about legal standards in this area. It should be noted that this authority controls and supervises the compliance with the provisions of labor law, which means that the advice provided thereby has relatively high authority.

It should be emphasized that free legal aid is complementary to the assistance provided by entities who professionally act as legal representatives for litigation purposes as, generally, only the latter entities can represent their clients in court and dispute proceedings.

Literature

Kowalski J., Lamentowicz W., Winczorek P., *Teoria państwa i prawa*, Warszawa 1981.

Makowski D., *Inspekcja Pracy jako instytucja państwowego nadzoru nad przestrzeganiem prawa pracy*, Łódź 2017.

Przywora B., *Normatywny model przedsądowej nieodpłatnej pomocy prawne w Polsce*, Warszawa 2019.

Redelbach A., Wronkowska S., Ziembiński Z., *Zarys teorii państwa i prawa*, Warszawa 1994.

Studnicki F., *Cybernetyka i prawo*, Warszawa 1969.

Studnicki F., *Przepływ wiadomości o normach prawa*, Zeszyty Naukowe UJ, Prace prawnicze 22/1965.

Ewelina Gierach[1]

Quality control of free legal aid

Abstract: The aim of the review is to draw up a definition of the "quality of free legal aid", provide an indication of the mechanisms of such control and review the effectiveness of these mechanisms in practice. The scope of research includes the applicable legal regulations as well as the analysis of the practice of their application. As part of the research, the following research questions were asked: (1) is it possible to lay down a unique definition of "the quality of legal aid?" (2) what quality control mechanisms for the provision of free legal aid are provided for by the applicable provisions? (3) what standards form the grounds for controlling free legal aid? How effective are the performed controls in practical terms? The study will primarily verify the following preliminary research hypotheses: (1) there is no legal definition of "the quality of free legal aid", (2) mechanisms for controlling the quality of free legal aid have been provided for by the provisions of the Free Legal Aid Act, as well as result from the provisions of corporate and local government laws, (3) the applicable provisions determine the standards of quality control, but its effectiveness depends heavily on the entities responsible for this control.

Keywords: free legal aid, professions of public trust, legal aid

1. Introduction

The right to obtain free legal assistance from a professional lawyer is part of the constitutional right to a court[2]. The guarantee of the use of legal services also by persons whose material situation does not allow them to cover the costs of such assistance is, however, not limited to ensuring access to professional services. It also includes ensuring their quality. Importantly, however, there is no legal definition of "quality of legal advice provided". This study aims to formulate a definition

1 Cardinal Stefan Wyszyński University in Warsaw. ORCID: 0000 0002 2689 786X.
2 See e.g. the judgment of the CT of 29 August 2006, SK 23/05, on this topic: O. Halub-Kowalczyk, *Sformalizowany model dostępu do nieodpłatnej pomocy prawnej na etapie przedsądowym w Polsce*, Wrocław 2019, p. 95 et seq.

of the "quality of free legal aid provided", to identify mechanisms for such control and to verify the effectiveness of the functioning of these mechanisms in practice.

The following research questions were posed: is it possible to formulate an unambiguous definition of "quality of free legal advice"; what mechanisms for controlling the quality of free legal advice are provided for in current legislation; what standards are used to control the free legal advice provided; what is the effectiveness of the controls carried out in practice?

The study will primarily verify the following preliminary research hypotheses:

- There is no legal definition of the "quality of free legal advice",
- The mechanisms for controlling the quality of free legal advice are provided for by the provisions of the Act on Free Legal Aid, as well as by the provisions of Companies and Municipalities Acts,
- The regulations in force determine the standards of quality control carried out, but its effectiveness depends to a large extent on the entities responsible for this control.

The study will cover the applicable regulations and analyze the practice in applying them. The basic methodology used is the dogmatic method. The study is based on the exegesis of legal texts and a review of the relevant literature on the quality of legal services. In addition, case law on the concepts concerned by the research problems will be analyzed.

2. Definition of free legal aid

According to the provisions of the Free Legal Aid Act; free legal aid includes: informing the entitled person of the legal State in force and of their rights or obligations, including in connection with pending preparatory, administrative, judicial or court-administrative proceedings; indicating to the entitled person how to solve their legal problem; drafting a draft letter on the above matters, excluding pleadings in pending preparatory or judicial proceedings and letters in pending court-administrative proceedings; free mediation; preparing a draft letter for exemption from court costs or appointment of an ex officio attorney in court proceedings or appointment of an advocate, legal adviser, tax adviser or patent agent in administrative court proceedings and informing about the costs of the proceedings and the financial risks of taking the case to Court (art. 3(1) of the Act on Free Legal Aid).

3. Entities providing free legal advice

The catalogue of entities entitled to provide legal aid is closed. Pursuant to art. 5(1) of the Act on Free Legal Aid, "free legal assistance shall be given in person by an advocate or a legal advisor and in particularly justified cases, upon their authorisation, by an advocate trainee or an advocate advisor". It is not irrelevant to the question of the quality of free legal advice that the law also allows legal assistance to be provided by a lawyer or tax adviser of a non-profit-making non-governmental organization (art. 11 of the Act on Free Legal Aid). Notably, the person providing free legal advice from a non-governmental organization does not have to be a professional (vocational) lawyer[3]. Pursuant to art. 11(3) of the Act on Free Legal Aid, in those legal aid points, the operation of which was entrusted to a non-governmental organization, legal aid may also be provided by: (1) a tax advisor – in the field of tax law, excluding tax cases related to the conduct of business activity; (2) a person who: (a) has a university degree and a master's degree in law or a foreign law degree recognized in the Republic of Poland; (b) has, at least, three years of experience in performing activities requiring legal knowledge directly related to the provision of legal assistance, (c) enjoys full public rights and has full capacity to perform legal activities, (d) has not been punished for an intentional crime prosecuted by public indictment or a fiscal crime. Moreover, it is worth noting that pursuant to art. 11(1)(2) of the Act on Free Legal Aid, non-governmental organizations are statutorily guaranteed a 50 % share in the legal aid points, which is why guarantees of high-quality advice provided by the indicated persons are so important.

4. The concept of quality of legal advice provided

The Act on Free Legal Aid does not define the term "quality of legal advice given". It only indicates the scope of legal services that can be obtained at the legal aid office, which is limited to legal information, legal advice and, to a limited extent, the drafting of letters. However, the provisions of the Act on Free Legal Aid do not define the minimum standards of services provided in this area. An analysis of the notion of "quality of the legal advice provided" leads to the conclusion that the defined "quality" can be considered on two levels. On the one hand, it is an objective – substantive assessment of the advice and opinions provided. On the other hand, it is a subjective feeling of the entitled person about receiving proper legal assistance. In this context, it is important that the rights holders' assessment of "adequate legal advice" includes, above all, non-substantive elements such as a friendly reception, comprehensible presentation of information, location of the office and legibility of the signposts, timeliness of the advice and explanation of the next steps to be taken[4]. It was the legislator's task to establish safeguards to secure both these aspects of the "quality" of free legal advice.

---

3 See M. Kaczocha, *Ustawa o nieodpłatnej pomocy prawnej oraz edukacji prawnej. Commentary*, Lex/el. 2016.

4 See *Evaluation of the Minister of Justice of the implementation of tasks in the field of free legal aid, free civic counselling and legal education for 2020*, Ministry of Justice 2021, p. 39, text available at: https://np.ms.gov.pl/aktualnosci/Ocena%20Minis tra%20Sprawiedliwo%C5%9Bci%20z%20realizacji%20zada%C5%84%20z%20zakr esu%20nieodp%C5%82atnej%20pomocy%20prawnej%20nieodp%C5%82atnego%20 poradnictwa%20obywatelskiego%20oraz%20edukacji%20prawnej%20za%202020%20 r.,40 (accessed: 30.10.2021).

5. Guarantees of quality of free legal advice provided

The provisions of the Act on Free Legal Aid do not explicitly indicate a catalogue of guarantees of the quality of free legal advice provided, however, a number of such safeguards can be deduced from the entirety of the Act's provisions.

The quality of the free legal assistance provided is undoubtedly guaranteed by the fact that it is entrusted to advocates and legal advisers, i.e., persons exercising professions of public trust. In particular, art. 5(1) of the Act on Free Legal Aid requires that the assistance is provided "in person". Based on this provision, replacing an advocate or legal adviser by a trainee advocate or trainee legal adviser, respectively, or by another lawyer employed in a law office, should be regarded as excluded. Only in particularly justified cases may advice be provided by authorized trainee advocates or legal advisers. However, the legislator has not specified when there is a "particularly justified case" and when it is therefore entitled to use the assistance of a trainee lawyer. This type of situation can undoubtedly include fortuitous circumstances and other insurmountable obstacles to providing legal assistance in person, e.g., the need to carry out activities related to the lawyer's or legal adviser's office[5].

The legal obligation to conclude a contract with the county (art. 6(1) of the Act on Free Legal Aid) is not irrelevant to the quality of the legal advice provided. The lawyer (legal adviser) provides legal aid in accordance with the concluded agreement, the exemplary elements of which are listed in art. 6.2.1-7 of the Act. This provision, by using the wording "in particular", does not limit the agreement's provisions to the indicated issues[6]. At the same time, there are no obstacles to the contract stipulating the rules of providing free legal assistance, reflected in the quality of these services.

The Act on Free Legal Aid guarantees free legal aid to eligible persons in a wide range of areas – from criminal law to tax, civil and family law. However, the act does not provide for the assignment of lawyers providing free legal assistance to a particular area of law. This creates a risk of low-quality legal advice provided when there is a need to provide legal assistance in an area not dealt with by a given advocate or legal advisor. In order to prevent this phenomenon, the legislator has provided in art. 8(9)(1) of the Act on Free Legal Aid that all or only selected lawyers on call may have a particular specialization. The specialization of on-call legal assistance is specified in particular by indicating the field of law or subject

---

5 See B. Paxford, R. Rynkurn-Werner, M. Wasylkowska-Michur, *Ustawa o nieodpłatnej pomocy prawnej oraz edukacji prawnej. Commentary*, Warsaw 2016, commentary to art. 5 nb. 1; J. Wegner, B. Wróblewski, *Prawo jednostki do nieodpłatnej pomocy prawnej*, "Przegląd Prawa Publicznego" 2021, no. 6, p. 11.

6 One of the obligatory components of the contract on provision of free legal assistance is to specify the rules of providing representation by an advocate or legal adviser in the event that he or she is unable to provide free legal assistance in person (art. 6(2)(6) of the Act on Free Legal Aid).

matter of free legal assistance provided during on-call hours, or by indicating the group of entitled persons to whom free legal assistance provided during on-call hours is specifically intended.

However, it is important to note that where the lawyer or legal adviser providing free legal assistance does not have the necessary expertise, they have the right to refuse assistance under art. 5(3) of the Act on Free Legal Aid. This provision is vital for protecting the interests of the lawyer's client and limiting the lawyer's liability for providing erroneous advice. In an age of legal inflation, requiring a lawyer to be knowledgeable in many areas of law is unreasonable. They should then provide the entitled person with information on other legal aid points in the county. Only when there is no other lawyer at the given point of free legal aid, information about other legal aid points in the county should be provided.

In addition, under art. 7(1) of Act on Free Legal Aid, the advocate or legal adviser providing free legal assistance is obliged to document in the free legal assistance card each case of provision of such assistance. The card shall contain, in particular, the following information: information about the notified case and the assistance provided, the area of law covered by the assistance, the category of the case, the form of assistance provided, the time spent on the assistance and the number of visits by the eligible person to the same case, general information about the eligible person concerning in particular age, sex, education, income, household and place of residence as well as data concerning the point, the person providing the assistance and the date on which the assistance was provided. The assistance card shall contain a section covering the opinion of the entitled person of the assistance supplied. The completion of this part of the assistance card by the entitled person, including the provision of a telephone number for further consultation, is subject to the consent of the entitled person. The assistance card shall not contain personal data of the entitled person that can indisputably identify the person (art. 7(1)). The assistance card shall be documented electronically via an ICT system.

Originally, the act on free legal aid excluded the possibility of providing free legal aid by means of remote communication. The coronavirus pandemic resulted in a completely new situation for both local governments and persons benefiting from free legal aid. Indeed, the introduction of the epidemic state, and before that the epidemic threat, resulted in many restrictions in access to services, including free legal aid services. However, people in need of legal assistance should be able to rely on free advice from a lawyer or legal adviser even during a pandemic, and often, especially during this period. Moreover, the time of the pandemic generates a large group of new beneficiaries of free legal aid. With this in mind, the legislator, based on art. 29 of the Act of 14 May 2020 on amending some laws on protective measures in connection with the spread of the Sars-Cov-2 virus[7], introduced a number of amendments to the Free Legal Aid Act, inter alia, facilitating

7 Act of 14 May 2020 amending certain laws on protective measures in connection with the spread of the Sars-Cov-2 virus, Journal of Laws of 2020, item 875.

the provision of free assistance during the epidemic. Based on art. 28a(1) of the Act on free legal aid, in the case of a state of epidemic emergency, an epidemic or the introduction of a state of emergency, the provision of free legal aid or free civic advice may be carried out by means of distance communication and outside the premises of the point. It cannot be overlooked that the fundamental remote form of advice introduced entails a risk of abuse both by the recipients of this assistance and by the providers of advice, who may, in the case of remote work, make wider use, for example, of the support of applicants. This creates the risk of reducing the quality of legal advice provided remotely.

Among the statutory guarantees of high-quality of free legal advice, it is also worth pointing out the control mechanisms for the performance of free legal aid tasks provided for in the Act. Pursuant to art. 7(5) of the Act on Free Legal Aid, the starost shall analyze the statements of the eligible persons concerning the legal aid provided by the free legal aid, taking into account the need to improve and enhance the quality of the free legal aid. By virtue of art. 11 (8) of the Act on Free Legal Aid, this body also controls the performance of the contract by the non-governmental organization. Moreover, pursuant to art. 12(1) of the Act on Free Legal Aid, the starost submits quarterly to the Minister of Justice, through the competent voivod, collective data on the performance of the tasks related to the provision of free legal aid in the province (powiat) by the end of the month following the end of the quarter. In the summary data for the following quarter, information on 3 % of assistance cards is permitted.

The entrustment of free legal advice to representatives of the public trust professions – advocates and legal advisers, as already mentioned-translates into the quality of the advice provided. The specific nature of the activities covered by these professions has led the legislator to guarantee the quality of these services. Among the features of the public trust professions are, inter alia, substantive qualifications and a high ethical level[8]. Detailed rules for exercising the legal professions of public trust have been regulated in individual so-called corporate laws. In the context of the quality of free legal advice provided by advocates and legal advisers, the provisions of two Acts are particularly important: the Act of 26 May 1982 – Law on Advocacy[9] and the Law of 6 July 1982 on Legal Advisers[10].

In order to guarantee an adequate quality of free legal advice, a distinction should be made between the two groups of provisions of the above-mentioned acts. Firstly, those which generally regulate the rules of practicing advocates and legal advisers in terms of the quality of legal services provided. In this area, the codes of ethics also play a significant role – the Code of Ethics for Advocates and

8 L. Grzonka, J. Kostrubiec, *Profession of public trust. Przyczynek do dyskusji*, "Studia Iuridica Lublinensia" 2007, No. 9, p. 25 et seq.

9 That is Journal of Laws 2020, item 1621.

10 That is Journal of Laws 2020, item 75.

Dignity of the Profession (the Code of Ethics for Advocates)[11] and the Code of Ethics for Legal Advisers[12]. Secondly, it is necessary to mention those provisions of the aforementioned Acts that relate directly to providing free legal advice. According to art. 3(5a) of the Law on Advocacy, the tasks of the advocates' self-government include: "cooperating with local self-government units in ensuring the provision of free legal aid as referred to in the Act of 5 August 2015 on free legal aid and legal education", while according to art. 58(12)(l), the scope of action of the Supreme Bar Council includes: "enacting regulations concerning: (...) the rules for the appointment of advocates for the provision of free legal aid referred to in the Act of 5 August 2015 on free legal aid and legal education and the documentation of the free legal aid provided". Analogous regulations are provided for in art. 41 and art. 60 of the Act on Legal Advisers.

Providing erroneous legal aid may expose professional lawyers to the risk of liability for damages. Indeed, a professional lawyer is subject to an annual obligation to pay a premium for third-party liability insurance (art. 8a of the Law on Advocates and art. 22^7 of the Act on Legal Advisers). Unlike professional legal advisers, persons providing legal assistance who do not have the status of a professional have not been obliged by the legislator to conclude a civil liability insurance contract for causing damage to a client. At the same time, the legislator did not explicitly exclude their liability for providing incorrect advice, only in Annex No. 2 to the Act, constituting a model statement of a person benefiting from legal aid, the following wording was included: "I hereby declare that I have been informed that any liability for damages of the person providing me with free legal assistance is excluded, except in the case of damage caused by willful misconduct"[13]. Such a solution should be critically assessed from the perspective of ensuring the quality of free legal advice.

6. Conclusions

Although the Act on Free Legal Aid does not provide a legal definition of the concept of "quality of free legal advice", nor does it explicitly indicate a broad catalogue of safeguards to ensure this quality, such safeguards can undoubtedly be found in its provisions. An analysis of the regulations in force in this area leads to the conclusion that a number of the guarantees envisaged serve to ensure legal advice of a high substantive level, which cannot always be assessed by the person

11 https://www.ora-warszawa.com.pl/wp-content/uploads/2018/04/Kodeks-Etyki-Adwokackiej.pdf (accessed 30.10.2021).

12 https://kirp.pl/etyka-i-wykonywanie-zawodu/etyka/kodeks-etyki-radcy-prawnego/ (accessed 30.10.2021).

13 For a critical discussion of this solution, see J. Wegner, B. Wróblewski, *The right of the individual to free of charge...*, p. 13.

using the legal service. There are also mechanisms aimed at obtaining the subjective opinion of the person entitled after receiving legal advice.

At the same time, it is notable that there is a lack of statutorily defined detailed indicators to assess the quality and effectiveness of the free legal aid system. Importantly, there is also a lack of possibility of substantive evaluation of the advice provided by other lawyers (so-called peer review)[14].

It would be worthwhile to establish in detail a uniform way of documenting the activities of those providing assistance. And most importantly, the law should contain a mechanism of accountability for failing to meet the quality of the assistance provided, resulting in deletion from the list of free legal aid service providers, or a periodic ban on entering into a contract to provide assistance under the scheme.

Literature

Evaluation of the Minister of Justice of the implementation of tasks in the field of free legal aid, free civic counselling and legal education for 2020, Ministry of Justice 2021, p. 39, text available at: https://np.ms.gov.pl/aktualnosci/Ocena%20Ministra%20Sprawiedliwo%C5%9Bci%20z%20realizacji%20zada%C5%84%20z%20zakresu%20nieodp%C5%82atnej%20pomocy%20prawnej%20nieodp%C5%82atnego%20poradnictwa%20obywatelskiego%20oraz%20edukacji%20prawnej%20za%202020%20r.,40 (accessed: 30.10.2021).

Grzonka L., Kostrubiec J., *Profession of public trust. Przyczynek do dyskusji,* "Studia Iuridica Lublinensia" 2007, No. 9.

Halub-Kowalczyk O., *Sformalizowany model dostępu do nieodpłatnej pomocy prawnej na etapie przedsądowym w Polsce,* Wrocław 2019.

Kaczocha M., *Ustawa o nieodpłatnej pomocy prawnej oraz edukacji prawnej. Commentary,* Lex/el. 2016.

Paxford B., Rynkurn-Werner R., Wasylkowska-Michur M., *Ustawa o nieodpłatnej pomocy prawnej oraz edukacji prawnej. Commentary,* Warsaw 2016.

Wegner J., Wróblewski B., *Prawo jednostki do nieodpłatnej pomocy prawnej,* "Przegląd Prawa Publicznego" 2021, no. 6.

14 The demand for the creation of such a mechanism to review the quality of free legal services provided was made in a submission to the Minister of Justice on 1 March 2017 by representatives of social organizations, members of the Council for Free Legal Aid and Legal Education, summarizing the year's activities and the necessary amendments to the Law on Free Legal Aid and Legal Education.

Ius, Lex et Res Publica
Studies in Law, Philosophy and Political Cultures

Edited by
Anna Jaron

Vol. 1 Anna Jaron: Socio-Economic Constitutional Rights in Democratisation Processes. An Account of the Constitutional Dialogue Theory. 2012.

Vol. 2 Stanisław Filipowicz: Democracy – The Power of Illusion. 2013.

Vol. 3 Teresa Dukiet-Nagórska (ed.): The Postulates of Restorative Justice and the Continental Model of Criminal Law. As Illustrated by Polish Criminal Law 2014.

Vol. 4 Agnieszka Kupzok: Enforcement of Patents on Geographically Divisible Inventions. An Inquiry into the Standard of Substantive Patent Law Infringement in Cross-Border Constellations. 2015.

Vol. 5 Alicja Jagielska-Burduk / Wojciech Szafrański: Legal Issues in Cultural Heritage Management. A Polish Perspective. 2016.

Vol. 6 Maciej Mataczyński (ed.): The Takeover of Public Companies as a Mode of Exercising EU Treaty Freedoms. 2017.

Vol. 7 Maciej Barczewski (ed.): Value of Information. Intellectual Property, Privacy and Big Data. 2018.

Vol. 8 Pawel Smoleń, Marcin Burzec: Introduction to Polish Tax Law. 2018.

Vol. 9 Łukasz Pohl, Konrad Burdziak: Judicial Interpretation of the 1997 Criminal Code Provisions on Self-Defence. 2019.

Vol. 10 Adam Szot: Judicial Review of Administrative Discretion. The Influence of Court Decisions on Administrative Actions. 2019.

Vol. 11 Michał Peno / Konrad Burdziak (eds.): The Concept of Modern Law. Polish and Central European Tradition. 2019.

Vol. 12 Leszek Leszczyński / Bartosz Liżewski / Adam Szot (eds.): Potential of Precedent in the Statutory Legal Order. 2019.

Vol. 13 Łukasz Bolesta: In Search of a Model for the Legal Protection of a Whistleblower in the Workplace in Poland. A legal and comparative study. 2020.

Vol. 14 Paweł Chmielnicki / Adam Sulikowski (eds.): New Perspectives on Legislation. A Comparative Approach. 2020.

Vol. 15 Marcin Burzec / Beata Kucia-Guściora / Paweł Smoleń: Agricultural Activity in Poland: A Fiscal and Legal Study. 2020.

Vol. 16 Magdalena Półtorak / Ilona Topa (eds.): Women, Children and (Other) Vulnerable Groups. Standards of Protection and Challenges for International Law. 2021.

Vol. 17 Josef Albert Fox: Die polnische Verfassung vom 3. Mai 1791. Hintergründe der Entstehung und der Außerkraftsetzung. Stellung Polens im Zeitalter der Aufklärung. 2021.

Vol. 18 Barbara Janusz-Pohl (ed.): Juvenile Justice Systems: Poland-Brazil-Portugal. 2021.

Vol. 19 Leszek Leszczyński: General Reference Clauses in the Judicial Process. Context of Legislative Intentions Interpretative Discretion. 2021.

Vol. 20 Francisco J. Campos Zamora: Das Problem der Begründung richterlicher Entscheidungen. Eine Analyse auf der Grundlage der Theorie der juristischen Argumentation. 2021.

Ius, Lex et Res Publica

Studies in Law, Philosophy and Political Cultures

Edited by

Barbara Janusz-Pohl and Anna Jaron

Vol. 21 Aneta Skorupa-Wulczyńska: Language Rights of the Citizen of the European Union. 2022.

Vol. 22 Mateusz Osiecki: International Legal Aspects of Aerial Terrorism. Methods of Law Enforcement in Avia-tion. 2022.

Vol. 23 Vladimír Sharp / Gabriela Blahoudková / Jakub Handrlica (eds.): Law, Pandemics and Ownership Restrictions. 2022.

Vol. 24 Piotr Kasprzyk / Anna Konert: Drones – Future of Aviation Law? Interference of Public Law in Private Law. 2023.

Vol. 25 Szymon Pawelec (ed.): Consensual Procedures in Criminal Law – Comparative Perspective. 2023.

Vol. 26 Dorota Pudzianowska: The Statelessness in Public Law. 2023.

Vol. 27 Bogusław Przywora / Aleksander Wróbel: Formalised Access to Pre-jurisdictional Free Legal Aid. Analysis based on Example of Ukraine, Poland, Great Britain and Sweden. 2023.

Vol. 28 Ewa Dawidziuk / Patricia Panero / Anna Tarwacka (eds.): Family, Law, and Society: from Roman Law to the Present Day. 2023.

Vol. 29 Marian Grzybowski / Bogusław Przywora / Aleksandra Syryt (eds.): Free Legal Aid, Theory, Legal Basis and Practice. European Standards. 2024.

www.peterlang.com

www.ingramcontent.com/pod-product-compliance
Ingram Content Group UK Ltd.
Pitfield, Milton Keynes, MK11 3LW, UK
UKHW041827031026
15587UKWH00002B/605

9 783631 904763